D1002191

MORAL SITUATIONS

MORAL SITUATIONS

N. Fotion

The Antioch Press
Yellow Springs, Ohio
1968

To Jan and Reid

CONTENTS

I. INTRODUCTION   1
The problem. Questions. Sketches of moral and moral-like situations.

II. GENERAL ASPECTS OF MORAL SITUATIONS   17
Agents, patients, and judges in moral situations. Humans and moral situations. Actions and conditions in moral situations. Non-moral situations.

III. GENERALIZATION AND REASON GIVING   33
Rules in moral situations. The functions of rules. Dangers in the use of rules. The role of value judgments.

IV. PERSONAL, SELF-INTEREST, SOCIAL, AND MORAL SITUATIONS   49
Strictly personal and moral situations. Personal and prudential situations. Self-interest and moral situations. Self-obligations. Political, social, and moral situations.

V. THE ROLES OF LANGUAGE IN MORAL SITUATIONS   70
Agent-centered uses of language. Patient-centered uses of language. Judge-centered uses of language. Relations between various uses.

VI. MAKING JUDGMENTS IN MORAL SITUATIONS   92
Justifying moral judgments. Formulating moral judgments.

VII. SUMMARY AND CONCLUSIONS   106

ANNOTATED BIBLIOGRAPHY   116

INDEX   125

I.
INTRODUCTION

1. The Problem

Although one may not be interested in the study of ethics, he *should* be. He should be interested, because he has had to face up to moral (or ethical) problems in the past and undoubtedly will have to face up to others in the future. Further, although he may not face up to certain moral problems, these problems will face him whether he likes it or not. Finally, even though no moral problem is facing him now, he still may be in a moral situation whether he realizes it or not. All this is to say that moral situations, and the problems they sometimes engender, are rather hard to avoid, so one might as well learn to deal with them.

The sketches of various moral situations which follow serve three purposes. First, they give some indication of how the study of ethics should begin. It should begin not at the level of theory but at that of the moral situation itself. Indeed it is from the analysis of a variety of moral situations that most of the theory in this study will arise. Second, these sketches help one in developing perspective. Insofar as a person sees only certain situations—his own primarily—as *typical* of all moral situations, he may miss much of the variety on the moral scene. Third, the sketches serve as an invitation to the reader to reflect upon his own experiences and to add two or three of his own sketches to the list. This exercise should tempt him to become involved in the process of thinking about moral situations, even if at the outset of the study his involvement is only minimal.

Before presenting the sketches themselves, some explanation is in order of why "What is a moral situation?" is to be the key question in this study. Recent work in the philosophy of ethics has tended to move away from asking relatively specific questions toward asking more general ones. Instead of asking, as was common several decades ago, questions such as "What does good (ought, right, or just) mean?"[1] it is now more common to ask such general questions as "What is the place of reason in ethics?"[2] or "What is the moral point of view?"[3] Presumably in answering these latter questions one would answer the former, since, for example, knowing about the moral point of view would necessitate knowing such specific things as the meaning of good—one concept among many which is used regularly in taking the moral point of view. If there are advantages in adopting a general approach in a study, the greatest advantage might lie in starting at the most general level possible. As will become clear in later chapters, questions such as "What is the place of reason in ethics?" and "What is the moral point of view?" are not general enough. They tempt us to look at the study of ethics through the eyes of only one of the participants in a moral situation and thereby limit our view of ethics. This temptation is avoided by asking and answering the question "What is a moral situation?" That is about as general as you can get.

2. Questions

In reading these sketches, the following questions might be kept in mind:

1. G. E. Moore, *Principia Ethica* (Cambridge: University Press, 1948, first published in 1903). "It [ethics] is an inquiry to which most special attention should be directed; since this question, how 'good' is to be defined, is the most fundamental question in all Ethics." p. 5.

2. Stephen E. Toulmin, *An Examination of the Place of Reason in Ethics* (Cambridge: University Press, 1953), pp. 1–5.

3. Kurt Baier, *The Moral Point of View* (Ithaca: Cornell University Press, 1958), pp. 187–213.

1. In which sketches are the participants facing moral *problems* in contrast to being merely in moral *situations?*
2. Are the roles or functions of all of the participants the same in each sketch?
3. Which sketches, if any, are non-moral in character? Or is it merely that certain aspects of some (or all) sketches are non-moral?
4. What function does the philosopher play in each, or any, of these sketches?
5. Do, or can the participants always give reasons for the decisions they make? When they do give reasons, are these reasons always of one type?

3. Sketches of moral and moral-like situations

SKETCH 1

Many Negroes live in Metro. Most of them live in homes and apartments that are not especially attractive when measured against the homes and apartments of non-Negroes. Other social and economic measurements show other differences as well. Negro parents in Metro have smaller incomes, less education, and fewer white collar jobs than do non-Negro parents. Further, Negro families tend to be larger. Because in many of these families both the father, if one is about, and the mother work, the children are free to do what they want. In more cases than not, this "freedom" gets them into trouble with the law. The crime rate among Negro youth is high. The illegitimacy rate is also high.

These and similar conditions worry many Metro citizens. Some worry about the high crime rate and think that the legal authorities ought to be more strict in enforcing the laws. Strict enforcement, they argue, will dam activities moving in illegal channels, forcing them to seek channels on a higher, legal, level. These people are concerned also about the costs, in tax dollars, of public assistance to support some Negroes (unwed mothers, the unemployed, etc.). Some of these same people worry over the threat of Negroes moving into the white neighborhoods. Aside from the fact that many of them simply dislike Negroes, what they fear most, as the Negroes move in, is that they will "bring with them their high crime rate and low moral standards."

Others worry because they feel the Negro is "discriminated against." It is true that the legal authorities in Metro see to it that public places such as restaurants, movie houses, and stores are properly integrated. Still, these people point out, even when a Negro family has the money to move into a suburban home, they find it next to impossible to do so. Further, even when a Negro has a good education he rarely is offered the kind of job a white person with the same educational achievement would be offered.

Oversimplifying at least to some extent, opinion has tended to become polarized in Metro. On the one side, there are people who see the Negro as *different* from the white in certain significant ways. These people see these differences as a threat to their own and the community's happiness. Further, these people deny that there is discrimination in such areas as employment. Even in those cases in which the Negro has a degree after his name, the employers in Metro claim that he actually knows less than the comparable white applicant. The employer does not speculate as to why this is so. He merely feels that he should, for the benefit of the company he represents, objectively assess the skills of those who apply. In this assessment, as a matter of fact, he finds that Negro applicants score lower than white ones. He therefore feels obligated to hire whites rather than Negroes. To do otherwise would be to discriminate against the whites and to encourage inefficiency in company operations.

On the other side are those who are sympathetic with the Negro dilemma. They do not deny the existence of at least some differences between the Negroes and the whites. They grant, for example, that the crime rate among Negroes is higher than it is among whites. Yet they explain this and other differences in terms of certain lacks of opportunity. Had the Negro been given the same opportunity in the past to develop his talents he would, they argue, in all likelihood also have a low crime rate. Thus this group tends to look at the Negro less in terms of his present condition, which admittedly is not a happy one, than in terms of a person who has been disadvantaged. The one side, then, thinks of the Negro as a person who is *different*, while the other as a *person* who is different.

SKETCH 2

Bill and Mary have been married now for several years. They have two children and many of the physical comforts. By most standards they are happily married. Their friends, and they too, partially attribute their happiness to their ability to think about satisfying each other's needs. In a word, they are both thoughtful. Bill, for example, knows how unpleasant certain tasks around the house are to Mary. Since they do not bother him especially, he has gotten into the habit of doing them for her. For her part, Mary knows how much Bill enjoys golfing. In order to share this interest, she has taken up the game herself; and on those occasions when Bill's friends are not around, Mary goes golfing with Bill. This pleases Bill immensely, since he would otherwise feel guilty about turning Mary into a "golf widow."

SKETCH 3

Cash was in trouble when the stock market slide turned into a steep slope. He not only lost most of his millions, he was also exposed as having been engaged in financial practices which were shady and even dishonest. One evening he was found in his office, a victim of suicide. Those attending his funeral included his wife, children, and his business partner.

SKETCH 4

Smith was also a suicide victim. He lived alone, had no relatives and an equal number of friends. Neighbors speculate that he was lonely and figured that life simply was not worth living.

SKETCH 5

It was several years after the Great Atomic War before it became clear how different things were going to be. At first people thought that the ratio would return to what it had been for as long as man knew about man. But instead of returning to a one-to-one ratio after The War, the ratio of female to male births increased gradually until it settled at three-and-one-half to one. The Conservative Party argued that, given time and research, ways would be found to return things to normal, and in the meantime The Old Law of one husband to one wife should be maintained. The Liberals were split on this question. Some argued for a legal limit on the number of wives a male should have. Some felt it should be four, while other less greedy souls felt that a limit of three would serve to solve most of the social and moral problems brought about by the new post-war ratio. Still other Liberals thought that it would be depriving both sexes of their freedom to put any restrictions on how many wives a man might have.

SKETCH 6

Many generations after The Great Atomic War another problem caused consternation among the "peoples" of the Galaxy. The trouble was that there were people and then there were *people*. By this time, the social and biological sciences had gathered certain data and had advanced to the point where no one could deny the existence of basic differences among people. Although there was overlapping so that, for example, some people from Planet S (The Silver Planet) had intellectual attributes to rival those of the inhabitants of Planet G (The Gold Planet), on the average G's inhabitants had a clear-cut statistical lead over S's on the latest BBC (Behavioral-Bio-Chemical) Tests. Similarly S's people showed a significant lead on these tests over the people from the Bronze Planet.

Bad feeling developed because earlier all of these peoples, the Gold, Silver, and Bronze, had come to accept the truth of the principle "All men are created equal." In view of the new data about the differences, this principle no longer rang true. The G Planet people argued that in view of the differences they ought to be given a larger share of the leadership roles in the Galactic Assembly and certain other privileges such as a higher reproductive quota. On the other hand, the B Planet people argued that as underprivileged people they should be given the benefit of the doubt through the introduction of special training programs which would tend to minimize the differences among the peoples. In any case, they agreed with the S people that "All men are created equal" was never intended to be taken literally, but rather to be interpreted as a guiding principle which could perhaps be expressed more clearly in the form "We ought to treat people as equals (before the law, etc.)." The G people countered with the following argument: Since the newly discovered differences among peoples were undeniable and biologically basic, the old rule of equality should be cast aside or seriously modified. Either that, they said, or we should continue to apply the old principle but realize that the inhabitants of the B and the S planets are *not* really people, humans, or men in the full senses of these words. Rather they should be thought of as people-like, human-like, or men-like creatures and be treated accordingly.

SKETCH 7

About this same time another problem developed, although, in a way, the solution was obvious once the problem itself was clearly formulated. The Great Atomic War had spawned many religious movements, among them one which believed that the war reflected something about the nature of man. Man, the Misanthropes believed, would continue to cause himself more grief than happiness in the long run. God evidently, for them, had made some horrible mistakes in creating man. The solution was to rid the cosmic scene of man. However, since the Misanthropes were a small group and had no technological power to do the job themselves, they hit upon the idea of example. After explaining their theory in great detail through the use of mass media, the whole group, except for a carefully selected rear guard, committed suicide at the Last Annual Misanthrope Convention. The example set by the Misanthropes inspired many of their sympathizers to suicide and even "murder." For a time it seemed as if the situation would get out of hand, for even some Philanthropes became despondent, and in one way or another many of them also did themselves in. A larger proportion of this group, perhaps 30 per cent, had no offspring. The Misanthrope Rear Guard labelled this group "cowardly" and "inauthentic" since, so the claim went, the Philanthropes knew what they should do but were not up to doing it. It took a long and emotional propaganda campaign to stop the suicides and restore the birth rate to an acceptable philanthropic level.

SKETCH 8

Emy Lou arranged for Beauregard to be her husband and lived to regret it. In some respects Beauregard was the ideal southern gentleman. His manners were impeccable and he never raised his voice to Emy Lou. In these respects, of course, Emy had no regrets. However, her regrets about the marriage began to take shape when the money their families gave them as wedding presents began to run low. In order to live in their accustomed manner, both had to work, Beauregard as a stock broker and Emy as a model. Actually she did not mind the work out of the home, provided Beauregard would help her some in the home. But Beauregard was too much of a "gentleman" even to think of having such duties in the home as caring for the children and housework. For her part Emy Lou was much too proud to say anything about the matter. So, as years passed, Emy Lou just wasted away.

SKETCH 9

Whatever the psychological and sociological reasons which led him to it, Adam rebelled against the prudish sort of upbringing to which he had been exposed as a child and a young man. But since he was a discriminating sort of fellow, he did not rebel as some do against all aspects of what he called "the conventional society." Besides, he saw no point in fighting society on all levels. It is better, he thought, to pick and choose one's issues. The issue he chose suited both his personality and pocketbook. He decided to champion the cause of certain body pleasures. To do this properly, he felt he needed a vehicle to disseminate his views. So he started publishing a magazine in which, among other things, he wrote articles arguing for and describing the subtleties of the body's pleasures. Wishing to offend as few and convert as many as possible to his views, he quite honestly and openly said what he was doing. He did not advocate the overthrow of any government, society, or even any institution within the society such as the church, schools, or the Junior League. Nor did he advocate that in seeking bodily pleasures people should deceive one another. On the contrary, he urged those who would follow him to learn to "relate" to one another honestly in order to enable them, in the long run, to enjoy larger amounts of the preferred type of pleasure than they would otherwise.

In spite of the financial success of his exciting magazine, Adam was not without his critics. He was called all sorts of unpleasant names and was thought, by these same name callers, to be thoroughly immoral. These critics pointed to what they considered to be the higher things or goals in life and criticized Adam for misleading the youth, and some who were not so young, into engaging in behavior which was immoral. Adam was unmoved by all this criticism. Of his critics he was quoted as saying, "I feel sorry for them. Because of their set views and their inhibitions they do not know what they are missing."

SKETCH 10

Albert, Billy, and Charlie thought themselves in agreement on the basic social and political problems of the day. After all, they had joined the Society for the Propagation of Individual Tendencies together and had agreed to follow SPIT's principles of individual freedoms as against the pressures of organized, socialized, and community life. But at the Society's meetings, where they really got to know one another, they realized how different their views really were.

Of the three, Charlie had to be rated the most "individualistic," since he was concerned with just one individual. For Charlie everyone, including his family, friends, business associates, and his employees, were objects to be used to make Charlie happy. It wasn't that Charlie was especially ruthless in dealing with others, although at times he could be, but that he just didn't have time to think of others. For him, making Charlie happy was a full-time job and simply took all his energies. In fact, he joined SPIT mainly because he realized how his own freedom was gradually being taken away from him through taxes, government regulation, and labor union pressures. For him, then, working with others was merely an expedient step toward achieving his own very personal ends.

Billy was something else again. In contrast to Charlie, he had a larger than "for me" sense of what was going on in the world. Indeed, this sense told him how badly things were going. In his work at City Hall he saw corruption all about him. Also he was impressed by the news of crime, riots, and wars throughout the country and the world. The world as far as he could see was "going all to hell." This being so, he felt that a person could do no better than to look out for himself until that time, if it ever did come, when the world would again come to its senses. He was fond of saying, "We are back in the jungle" and "This is war!" But taking his cue from some of the more radical theologians of the day, his favorite expression was "Morality is dead." It was dead, he thought, at least for the foreseeable future, so he preached and practiced the doctrine of self-survival.

Although it sounded different on the surface, Albert was never quite sure whether his views differed basically from Billy's. To be sure, Albert also took a dim view of world trends. But through SPIT and other groups he hoped to convince others to replace their wrong *moral* position with his correct one and not give up on morality altogether. Contrary to what Billy was saying, Albert could never understand what "Morality is dead" meant, unless it were to apply at a time when all men were dead. For Albert, even in times of chaos the morally right and wrong things could be distinguished. In chaotic times Albert agreed with Billy about following the principle of "Look after your own interests." But he wanted people, all people, to look after their own interests as part of the process of preserving and maintaining a high level of life. It was at this point that he thought Billy's position might be identical with his own. Since Billy talked about self-preservation to others, some of whom were not even his friends and would therefore not likely ever be in position to help him preserve his *own* life, Albert accused Billy not of abandoning morality altogether but rather of advocating a special brand of morality. "You too," Albert argued, "are concerned with the welfare of all mankind. Either that, or you are practicing some variation of Charlie's position and are only interested in yourself."

However, on another point Albert's position was clearly more developed than Billy's. His doctrine of looking after one's own interests applied not only in times of chaos but in so-called normal times. For him, looking after one's own interests was just humanly more fulfilling and efficient. If everybody, he felt, competed for his own interest on a fair basis with others, rather than depending on them for help, in the long run there would be more happiness. Albert thought that benevolence, except insofar as it helped another develop his self-interest, was misguided. When misused, he felt, benevolence led to indolence, loss of self-respect, lower production of human goods, and similar miserable conditions. On moral grounds, he argued, we should do all we can to make people self-sufficient and interested in their own interests.

SKETCH 11

If one totalled up his winnings and losses, Simon appeared not to have been a very smart gambler. Or maybe it was just bad luck. Whatever it was, it always seemed as if he lost more money than others at gambling. Win or lose, though, it didn't matter much because he usually had more money than he knew what to do with. Besides, gambling was a kind of game with him and he simply enjoyed playing it. Indeed, he thought, most games cost money, for equipment or tickets, so his was really no different from golf, bowling, and other games. Besides, who knows, with gambling one might even win a bundle.

All this was well and good prior to Sue's arrival on the scene. Her charm distracted Simon from his favorite game long enough to result in marriage and a bit later in the birth of their first child. In time a second child was born. But distractions being what they are, Simon returned to his favorite game and proceeded, of course, to lose money again. Now with a wife, two children, payments on the house, the car, furniture, and the lawn mower there was not only no extra money for Simon's little game, but since he was a loser at gambling, certain bills were just not being paid. At first Sue *asked* Simon to quit gambling and Simon *promised* solemnly to do so. But far from quitting, he only *lied* to Sue. In time Sue discovered that nothing had changed, so now she *pleaded* with Simon. After a while she *threatened* to leave him unless he quit gambling.

Meanwhile Simon's friend Sam *chided* him about his gambling. "Must," he said, "the boy still play his little games?" Even Simon's boss, a Mr. Silver, got on his back when he observed how Simon's work was being affected by his domestic problems. Mr. Silver simply *ordered* Simon to quit gambling.

A week later Sam *reported* to Sue that Simon had passed up two golden opportunities to make bets. Sue's comment, only it wasn't really a comment but rather a *sigh* of relief, was "Thank God!" In the future there were other so-called golden opportunities but, with some trivial exceptions, Simon passed them up. Needless to say, Simon and Sue lived happily ever after.

SKETCH 12

Rouser had a way with words. In fact, his persuasive powers were so great that using them became a way of life with him. At first he used his powers to talk *others* into doing what he thought should be done. But "what he thought" is somewhat misleading, since he rarely did any thinking prior to loosing his persuasive powers on others. "What he thought" actually came down to "what he wanted at that moment." Yet whatever he wanted, he found, could be talked about in a way so as to make it seem morally right and just to others. On the occasion of the concerted Negro drive to move Mr. and Mrs. Black into The Ivory Hills neighborhood, Rouser convinced his neighbors that it would be a mistake to let this drive succeed. "It's premature," he urged, pointing to the "cultural gap" which he felt existed between his group and the Blacks. Besides, he noted, the Blacks had nine children. In addition, Mr. Black's parents planned to live with their son and his family. "This is not just a family move into the neighborhood," Rouser noted with a smile, "this is a *tribal* invasion."

The point at which Rouser's cutting and emotional persuasive talk became a way of life with him was when even *he* began to believe what he was saying. On those rare occasions when he was tempted to sit down in order to think through his problems, he found himself standing up and making a speech instead. In due time, he was giving speeches not only when he was actually giving speeches but when he was talking to his wife, children, friends, and even himself. In the end, to no one's surprise, he became very powerful politically.

SKETCH 13

It was the most amicable divorce you could imagine. Indeed, it was so amicable it left everyone wondering why it was even necessary. Even after the divorce, they often saw one another and continued, as they did before their divorce, to enjoy one another's company. In fact, both before and after the divorce, they got along together better than most couples who stay married (admittedly this may not be a very strong point). Yet for Alice and Alan all this was not enough. They considered themselves to be special people and, to that extent, they demanded more from marriage than amicability and what they sometimes called a "conventional marriage relationship."

In point of fact, it was Alice who took the first step which led eventually to the dissolution of the marriage. Before that, both had become aware of certain temperamental differences which tended to separate them. Alice, the more outgoing of the two, thrived on contacts with other people, while Alan was quite content to live primarily within the wife-husband relationship. There were other differences in taste and manner of doing things, all of which took their toll of a relationship which looked so promising when they first met. In spite of these differences, Alan loved, or at least thought he still loved, Alice. However, Alice was quite certain she no longer loved Alan, and this realization was the immediate cause of her setting in motion the divorce proceedings. Alan, not surprisingly, was upset by this turn of events but did not want to hold Alice "captive" in a relationship which was obviously deteriorating. For the sake of her happiness, and perhaps even his own in the long run, he agreed to the amicable divorce.

For her part Alice would not even have asked for the divorce had not the situation been *quite* the way it was. In the first place, there were no children involved to complicate the matter. Nor was there the complication of parental disapproval or upset, since both Alice and Alan had long since been orphaned. Third, Alice was certain that Alan was emotionally stable enough not to be seriously disturbed or literally destroyed by her request for a divorce. Fourth, she knew that the divorce proceedings themselves would not lead to rancor. She knew herself and her husband well enough to predict accurately how each would react to the situation. Understandably, neither one was totally unemotional about the proceedings but, by and large, they managed to contain their emotions and discuss rationally what they should do. Had they not had the training and education which they had, they perhaps would not have been so rational about the whole business. But they had in fact a good deal of understanding about what had happened to them, thanks to a great deal of reading they had done on these matters, and thanks also to their concern about one person's relationship with another insofar as they had often helped others straighten out their affairs. Fifth, Alice and Alan had now been married for several years and there was no longer any question, not even in Alan's mind, of the unfortunate direction their marriage was taking. Sixth, they were both still young enough to look forward to the prospect of remarriage. Especially with Alice this was an important consideration. If she were to wait much longer—she was now twenty-five— she felt her chances of remarrying in time to have the children she wanted badly would not be very good. These factors, plus those already mentioned—her lost love for Alan, their temperamental and taste differences, and their desire for something more emotional out of marriage than most people demand—were enough to justify her asking Alan to release her.

In agreeing to the release, Alan shared with Alice a certain cluster of other attitudes toward their situation. In particular, they both felt generally that divorces should be discouraged. And if it were not for their *special* circumstances they would not have sought a divorce. They did, then, obtain their divorce for reasons which most people could not understand or countenance. In time Alice re-married, had two children, and lived the kind of fulfilled life she was seeking. Alan was less fortunate. He was happy that Alice had found happiness, but he himself never did find another person with whom to achieve this state.

SKETCH 14

"I know I don't deserve a C but can't you change a grade—just this once? Unless I get a C, I won't be able to graduate." When the professor answered, "But if I change your grade I will have to change at least fifteen others from D to C," the student had a ready answer. "But I won't tell anyone," he said.

II.
GENERAL ASPECTS OF
MORAL SITUATIONS

1. Agents, patients, and judges in moral situations
Looking at the sketches from the previous chapter, it seems obvious enough that *people* are involved in moral situations. Not quite so obvious is the nature of their involvement. Traditionally philosophers have distinguished between the agent and what is sometimes called the patient in a moral situation. The agent "is always a person who is acting or has acted or is contemplating action."[1] The patient, on the other hand, might be thought of as someone for whom the agent is acting, has acted, or is contemplating action. Conceived as such, these concepts are surely useful in characterizing roles which people play in at least some types of moral situations, but they are too narrow in scope to be completely satisfactory.

In certain types of situations there is little or no problem in identifying agents and patients. When a husband (Sketch 2) does something around the home for his wife, the former is the agent while the latter is the patient. Depending on the circumstances, a husband can be the agent one moment and the patient the next. However, it is not quite so clear who is the agent (or the patient, for that matter) in a situation in which the female-to-male birth

1. William Frankena, in D. D. Runes, *The Dictionary of Philosophy* (New York: Philosophical Library).

ratio changes from one to one, to three-and-a-half to one (Sketch 5). Presumably anyone who has the authority to bring about a change in the rules of marriage can be thought of as an agent, although others actually participating in the rites of marriage may also be agents (and patients). It is even less clear whether to call a person an agent when he fails to act because he is unaware of his obligations to act (Sketch 8). In the somewhat similar situation of the "friend" who consciously refuses to help us when we are in need, there is no question as to what to call him. He can be called an agent, as well as more colorful names, because his refusal is a kind of action which helps keep our needs from being satisfied. But the one who is literally unaware of his responsibilities to act may be something else again. Such a person's lack of awareness of his obligations to help his wife around the home, even though she is a "working-wife," for example, makes for a moral situation or problem simply because he has not identified himself as the agent. Still, such a failure on his part would hardly seem enough to keep him from earning the title of agent, or at least potential agent. It is not as if he were totally incapable of recognizing his responsibilities. Rather it is more a matter of his overlooking or forgetting to do his duty in *one* situation. In any case, some people would consider him (almost) as blamable for his omission as they would the friend whose omissions include giving help to his friends (but who nevertheless somehow always manages to receive help from them). The concept of agent, then, can apparently be thought of as applicable to moral situations not only when someone has acted, is acting, or is contemplating action but in other situations as well. In thus broadening this concept to include the person who is consciously inactive and even perhaps the one who is unaware of his responsibilities to act, it may very well be that one or more agents can be found in each moral situation. However, there is no need to take a definite stand on this matter. It is enough for now merely to note the general presence of agents in moral situations and to have some understanding of the roles they play in such situations.

The concept of patient also needs to be broadened. As the word "patient" suggests, a person in a moral situation can be likened to someone in a medical situation. As such, a patient would be someone who is in need of help and, presumably, is either about to or is in the process of receiving it. In this sense of patient, both the old lady about to cross the street as a boy scout troop happens by and the parent who is receiving affection from his children are candidates as patients in moral situations. But in this medical sense of patient there would be many moral situations in which the concept would be inapplicable, for some of these situations are moral not because someone needs help and is being offered it, but because his needs are deliberately not being satisfied or even because he is being hurt deliberately. These "patients" are patients only in the sense that they are suffering. In this broadened sense of the word, a patient in a moral situation is someone who is being acted upon morally or immorally, or is not being acted upon but should be. In broadening this concept, it may be, as with the concept of agent, that at least one patient can be found in each moral situation. However, again as with the concept of agent, there is as yet no need to take a stand on this issue.

Although important, the next category of people to be identified as involved in moral situations does not appear to be applicable to each moral situation. Like the concept of patient, words used to describe this category are not completely satisfactory. The two which most closely hit the mark are "critic" and "judge." The word "critic" is somewhat unsatisfactory because it has connotations of an unfavorable judgment although, of course, in literary circles a critic can and has even been known to say nice things about what he is evaluating. At any rate, it is in this latter sense of evaluating, either favorably or unfavorably, that "critic" most closely approximates an important category of a moral situation.

The trouble with the concept of judge is that in most contexts it suggests the weighing of consequences or reasons before making a decision. Weighing of reasons may be something we want to encourage in moral situations, yet it is not something which always or even very frequently takes place in these situations. To a lesser extent "critic" has this same fault. The point is this: At a certain stage in a moral situation someone must judge, decide, determine, select, opt for, or simply arbitrarily pick one alternative rather than another. And if this person simply arbitrarily picks, it sounds strange to call him the critic or judge. Yet for want of better words, these are the ones I shall use to characterize the individual who chooses one rather than another alternative, no matter how rationally or irrationally he does this.

Now why may not the critic or judge be universally present in moral situations the way the agent and patient presumably are? The primary reason is that once the judge has "judged" the situation, the action which results from the "judgment" (choosing with or without reasons) may become habitual. It may therefore become somewhat inappropriate to talk of a judge or critic as being involved in the moral situation, at least at this stage. Even when someone is acting habitually, as might be the case with the loyal husband after many years of marriage, he can still be spoken of as the agent and his wife the patient in this situation. Yet it might not be appropriate to talk of him as *the* or *a* judge any longer.

Three points should be made about the concepts of agent, patient, and judge (or critic) to avoid misunderstanding. First, as was already noted about the first two of these concepts, more than one person in any moral situation can play any one of these roles. Thus the judge in a situation can be one person, a panel of persons, or the whole population—as would be the case in a democratically run society. Second, one person can, although he need not, play more than one role in any one situation. Quite often, in fact, the judge and the agent are one and the same person, as would be the case when someone *decides* to *take part* in an effort to settle a Negro family (the patients) in an all white neighborhood. In fact, as I shall argue in the next chapter, it is possible to play all three roles, not only in different situations, but even in the same situation. Third, the three categories of people are by no means the only ones involved in moral situations. If A promises B to help C, A may very well be a judge in this situation, and he surely is the agent. Equally, C is surely the patient. But what status does B have here? He might also be thought of as a patient except for the fact that A's hoped-for actions are not really directed at him but rather at C. It is at least arguable then that none of the categories already presented fits B. Nor do the three categories of agent, patient, and judge seem to fit completely people who play such roles in moral situations as those of a teacher or advisor. So, although the categories of agent, patient, and judge in moral situations may turn out on later analysis to be universal, as they surely are very important, the presence of other categories of people in these situations is an indication of a degree of complexity beyond what might at first be supposed.

An analysis of these other categories and their complicating effects will follow in later chapters. However, in order to avoid confusion, it is advisable to discuss without delay still another concept or category of people—that of the philosopher of ethics—and to distinguish it from the category of critic or judge. One of the reasons for confusion here is the varied roles of the critic or judge. As was already noted, the judge often is the same person as the agent, since he can both decide what to do in a specific situation and then proceed to carry out his own decision. When the critic actually carries out the decision or perhaps plays the role of a commander (as a general in the army might) he is in a very real sense directly involved *in* the moral situation, since his decision is the one which counts. However, others may judge or be critics *of* the situation and literally not be involved in or be a part of the situation. They may be friends of the ones in the situation, bystanders, historians who are looking at what happened in retrospect, or any number of other types of person. In this bystander sense of critic, the critic is not necessary to any specific moral situation, as the involved critic might very well be. Nevertheless, since he too judges the situation, albeit in a detached fashion, I shall use the words critic and judge to cover both the involved and the non-involved type.

The concepts of critic and judge, especially critic, have still another connotation. Thus far a critic has been mainly conceived as someone who judges some specific moral situation. Yet critics can make judgments not only about a specific situation, such as whether Smith should return the money he borrowed now or later, but of ones more general in nature, such as how minority groups should be treated or even about the direction a whole society is going. It is when the critic starts to think of the big and basic moral questions that the roles of the critic and the philosopher tend to become confused, since the philosopher is *also* supposed to be concerned with big and basic questions. In whatever way the distinction between the general critic of society, on the one side, and the philosopher of ethics, on the other, is to be made finally (see Chapter VII) note should be taken of the different sorts of questions they seem to be asking. The critic of man or society, whom I shall call the moral or social thinker, asks such questions as: "Under what circumstances, if any, am I obligated to kill another human being?" "Is freedom more basic than equality?" "Are we losing our basic values?" or "Should we seek new ones?" If the kind of question being asked in this work is typical of the sort philosophers ask, then, at least on the face of it, the social thinker and the philosopher are engaged in two different sorts of tasks. The overall question being asked here, it will be recalled, is "What is a moral situation?" To be sure, philosophers of ethics have not been involved in asking just this particular question. They have also asked such questions as "What is a moral judgment?" "What is the meaning of good (right, ought)?" and "How do moral judgments differ from scientific ones?" Yet all these questions at least *look* different from all of the questions cited above as typical of the kind the moral or social thinker asks.[2] Of course, the fact that they look different proves nothing, since once one has completely answered the typical philosopher's question he may have answered those of the social thinker also. But this possibility is highly debatable and, as I shall argue later, is downright dubious. So for the time being, at least, the philosopher of ethics will be taken as a person who is playing a role different from those of the agent, the patient, and the critic. His role is different not only because he asks different sorts of questions from the critic (and as a philosopher he is not acting as an agent or being acted upon as a patient) but also because he is neither *in* the moral situation as are the agent and patient, nor is he the judge *of* that situation as is the critic. The philosopher, in contrast to the agent, the patient, and even the critic who are all *a part of* the situation, is *apart from* it. His role is to sit back, as it were, and ask such questions as "What are the elements of a moral situation?" and make such distinctions as those of the agent, patient, and critic. By asking and answering these questions, of course, the philosopher may help the participants, especially the critic; but still his role is distinct.

What has just been said about the philosopher's role in, or apart from, moral situations should not be misunderstood. The critic, it will be remembered, can at the same time also be the agent and even perhaps the patient. In talking about critics, agents, patients, and philosophers of

2. Bernard Mayo, *Ethics and the Moral Life* (New York: St. Martin's Press, 1958). "We can express the differences between the three types of activity by saying that the actors are merely acting, they are not thinking what the are doing; the critics are not doing anything, but are thinking about what is done; in particular, they are making comments or criticisms in the light of criteria or principles. Finally, the philosophers are neither doing nor thinking about what is being done; they are thinking about the criteria or principles of the critics, about the concepts used in their thinking. While critical thinking is once removed from practice, philosophical thinking is twice removed." pp. 10–11.

ethics, what really is important are *functions,* not *labels.* The question is then not whether so and so can be labelled critic rather than something else, but what functions does so and so perform in moral contexts. A person may be a philosopher of ethics *and* a critic. In theory he might very well play all four roles in the same situation. What would be especially important if he were such a multiple-role player would be for him to keep his various roles straight. It might not do to have Smith judge in the patient's favor one time, when he just happens to be the patient, and in the agent's favor another time, when he just happens to be the agent. One's role as a judge or critic has been observed at least occasionally to be a function of what other roles a person plays in the moral situation. As a patient, as the possible recipient of a promotion, for example, Smith might very well judge himself to have more than earned the promotion. He might also play down or totally ignore certain of his own failings. Yet later, when playing the agent's role as an administrator, he might not be so tempted to ignore these same failings in others. Some awareness of role might help to lessen such errors in judgment. It would also not do to be unaware of the possibility of the distinction between the critic and the philosopher of ethics and therefore to assume uncritically that an answer to such philosopher's questions as "What is a moral situation?" and "What does *good* mean?" leads directly to general ethical and moral truths of the kind the moral or social thinker type of critic would be interested in.

In summary, an initial look at the question "What is a moral situation?" has shown people to be playing a wide variety of roles in moral situations. Some, those playing the role of agent, patient, or judge, have a more direct involvement than others (e.g., the observer of a moral situation). The philosopher of ethics, on the other hand, evidently is not involved in the moral situation in either the direct or the passive sense. Nor is he involved in the moral situation by way of taking an overall look at the moral realm in order to try to put the specific moral situation into some moral or social framework. The philosopher, in short, is not a social thinker. Rather, he is a thinker about different sorts of questions, such as "What is a moral situation?" and "What is the meaning of *good?*" One who is a philosopher can, of course, and no doubt must, play other roles. Thus he does become directly involved in moral situations as a citizen, parent, advisor, friend, or what have you. Insofar, however, as he plays his philosophic role he seems to be apart from, rather than a part of, the moral situation.

2. *Humans and moral situations*

Although it may have seemed trivially true to say at the outset that people (humans) are involved in moral situations, it is by no means obvious that they are the only ones so involved. Among those who believe in God, He is said to be morally good.[3] In fact, His moral character is often taken as following from His perfection. Even among non-believers the talk is sometimes in terms of "If He did exist, he would have acted in such and such a way (morally)"; and since, in their eyes, there is so much evil on earth, a morally good God must not exist. Clearly this sort of talk emphasizes God's (possible) involvement in the moral situation of creation as an agent. But God's involvement as an agent, as a creator, can hardly be separated from His involvement as a judge.[4] God, if He exists, would hardly be in a position to take orders from Someone Else and, even if needed and He had Heavenly Advisors, presumably it would be up to Him to evaluate this advice, and then act upon it. So God as an agent would also have to be a judge. But if God can become involved in moral situations as an

3. In his Meditations (4th) Descartes says: "For first, I recognize that it is impossible for God ever (43) to deceive me, since in all fraud and deception there is some kind of imperfection. And although it seems that to be able to deceive is a mark of (acumen,) (subtlety,) or power, nevertheless to wish to deceive testifies without question to weakness or malice, which could not be found in God." (Trans. by Lawrence J. Lafleur, New York: Library of Liberal Arts.)

4. Mayo, *op. cit.,* p. 62.

agent and judge, presumably angels (if they exist) and physical creatures somewhere other on the evolutionary ladder than where man is, who also exhibit the attributes of agency and judging, can also become so involved. One has either the choice here of extending the concepts of person to cover these other creatures and then say only persons are involved in moral situations, or of admitting that others besides "humans" or "persons" can be involved in moral situations as agents. However one does it, it would seem misleading at best to say, "morality applies to human beings, not to flaccid seaweed. Neither does it apply to angels, or to raving or even silent lunatics."[5]

It is even more misleading when the status of patients in moral situations is in question. Presumably God and angels could in principle be the recipients (patients) of actions forthcoming from human agents. Of course these patients can also play the agent's role. But other patients need not, since they may not possess the requisite powers to do so. A helpless child can be the recipient of someone's action. So can an adult who himself is incapable of acting and judging—such as a mentally defective person. Creatures somewhat higher or lower on the evolutionary or developmental scale than humans might also be recipients of moral attention (Sketch 6) although it is not clear just how low one can go and still treat the recipient of an action as an object worthy of moral attention. Would men-like creatures barely able to develop a language qualify as patient-candidates? How about men-like creatures just below that level? How about seaweed? Whatever the lower and upper limits, it would appear that the spectrum of creatures who would qualify as patient-candidates could be broader than the spectrum for agents and judges; and that both spectrums could extend to creatures beyond what we would normally consider to be humans or persons.

5. George Marcus Singer, *Generalization in Ethics* (New York: Alfred A. Knopf, 1961), p. 295.

3. Actions and conditions in moral situations

Referring back again to the sketches of Chapter I, not only are such concepts as agent, patient, and critic useful in characterizing moral situations generally, but so also are those of *action* and *condition*. In fact, as was already noted, the concept of agency is tied necessarily to action. The husband *helps* the wife *do chores* around the house, the mayor *takes steps* to solve a segregated situation, the man *commits suicide,* and so forth. Even in the case in which there is an omission of some action, as there would be if someone thoughtlessly forgets to carry out his duties to help his wife around the house, it is just the omission of the *action* which helps make the situation moral.

As to the concept of condition, it is not obviously implied by the concept of patient, as action is by agency, but, nevertheless, it is still tied in with it. If the agent is successful in carrying out his duty, the patient or recipient is not just literally on the receiving end of some action. Rather his condition is changed typically in a way which can be evaluated good or bad. Now what changes of condition in a patient are good or bad is not strictly speaking a question which will be answered here. Nor strictly speaking is it part of the present task to identify who are the patients in a (moral) situation. Both questions are ones answered as a part of the more general question of how one should judge and respond to a specific or general moral situation. The question being dealt with here is not about what we should do to whom in a moral situation, but instead what is a moral situation. Still, although it is not appropriate to answer the question of who specifically *are* patients, let alone how are they rightly or wrongly affected, it does seem proper to look for characteristics which generally help to define what a patient is. The concept of agent, for example, implies power or ability to act, plus freedom of action. Are there then similar characteristics for the patient, aside from those already mentioned of a creature which is the recipient (or potential recipient) of some action and is affected in a way which can be evaluated good or bad? Again referring to the earlier discussion of patients, some philosophers would amend or add to this characterization of patient by substituting "human" in place of "creature."[6] But such an amendation would seem to reflect less the answer to the question of what is a moral situation, and more what we actually value morally—humans and/or their condition.

This latter point can be appreciated when it is recalled that other societies, and even people in our own, argue for the moral reverence not only of humans or human life, but of other creatures and life in general. Differences of opinion as to who or what is a moral patient and how such a patient can be affected thus suggest that it might be best to keep the concept of patient *open-ended* and to decide these questions on moral grounds rather than to arbitrarily define certain creatures or even objects in general out of the moral realm in advance. It would appear best, then, to proceed cautiously and not list any other characteristic beyond those already listed as defining the concept of patient.

4. Non-moral situations

Enough has been said in answer to the question "What is a moral situation?" to suggest still other aspects of the answer to it. Until now the analysis of moral situations themselves, in particular the analysis of the sketches presented in Chapter I, yielded the categories of agent, patient, judge, action, and condition. Such an analysis highlighted also the detachment of the philosopher of ethics from these situations—a detachment suggested from the philosopher's failure to make his appearance as one of the characters in the moral sketches or situations. However, an understanding of what a moral situation is can be gained not only by a direct look at these situations, but also by

6. *Ibid*, pp. 294–295.

contrasting them, and the categories uncovered in them, to non-moral situations.

The kind of non-moral situations I have in mind are scientific (or empirical), religious, aesthetic, prudential, political, and social situations. Some of the situations of contrast will receive attention in later chapters. Yet because one of the questions to be discussed in the next chapter concerns the use of scientific information in a moral situation, the contrast of the moral to the scientific situations needs to be made now.

What, then, is a scientific (or empirical) situation? Initially the question sounds odd. It does not sound like the kind of question a philosopher of science would ask. He would more likely ask "What is a scientific judgment?" or something of the kind. But I think it is merely strange *sounding* rather than *really* strange or wrong to ask what a scientific situation is. The reason for asking the comparable question in ethics helps to show why. That question, "What is a moral situation?" was taken as the main and starting-point question because of the broadness of its scope. The intent was and is to narrow the scope once the broad-scope question has served its purpose of giving perspective to the general field of ethics. And indeed the what-is-a-moral-situation question has already served to avoid committing one kind of mistake. Had the basic question been "What is a moral judgment?" the temptation would have been to place greater emphasis on the roles of the judge and perhaps the agent to the neglect of the patient, and thereby lead to a loss of perspective. This loss of perspective would then have led to making such misleading claims as "Morality is a human activity" more plausible sounding, since the roles of the agent and the judge are more typically human than is the "role" of the patient.

Now the same gain in perspective may be the reward in asking a general question first about non-moral areas. To ask the question "What is a scientific or empirical situation?" is to ask a question broad enough to include the roles of the scientist and what he studies, just as to ask "What is a moral situation?" is a broad enough question to include in its scope the roles of the judge and what he studies (e.g., the agent, patient, action, and condition).

When one looks at the two questions together, pairing them up as it were, the roles of the scientist and the judge in the scientific and moral situations respectively seem to be roughly comparable. To be sure, differences will appear in the way they make their determinations of the situation, but both can be asked to develop theories, assess types of problems, and even make judgments about specific situations. Where there seem to be obvious differences between the two situations is in *what* the scientist and the judge assess. In the same sense in which the judge in a moral situation can identify agents and patients, the scientist cannot do so in scientific situations. After a fashion, talk of agents and patients can be adapted to scientific talk in terms of the concepts of cause and effect. But the concept of an agent, it will be remembered, implies freedom of action. One would hardly want to talk of a billiard ball as a cause (agent) acting freely. But there are even more fundamental differences between the two types of situations. In both, the concepts of action (or at least motion) and condition are applicable. A scientist can talk about the motion of the billiard ball and the condition in which it leaves a second billiard ball. He can also talk of how one person's actions have effects upon others. But whereas the scientist talks of what *has* happened, the moralist (the judge) talks about what *ought* to have happened; whereas the scientist talks of what is the case or what is happening, the moralist talks of what ought to be happening; and, finally, whereas the scientist talks of what will be the case or will happen, the moralist talks of what ought to be the case or ought to happen. Whereas, then, typically the scientist's talk is in terms of "has" (or "was") "is" and "will," the moralist's is in terms of "ought." Things are not that clear cut, of course. A scientist functioning as a scientist can say, if things go right, "We ought to have the meter read 100.0 units at 10 o'clock." But here the "ought" does not mean literally that it would be good (best) if it did happen, but rather that the prediction is that it will reach 100.0. On the other side, expressions can be found in moral situations which at least sound like those belonging to the scientist's realm, but which are still properly moral. One such, which at least in some contexts is used as a moral claim, is "All men are equal" (Sketch 6). It could be construed as a descriptive, that is a scientist's, claim since it speaks in terms of "are" ("is") rather than "ought," "right," or "good." Further, it could be argued that "equal" is also a scientist's word, since we do apply it in contexts in which we measure equal times and distances. With humans, "All men are equal" could be construed to mean that each man has one and only one soul and in this sense is equal; or perhaps that so-called races of people, blacks, whites, reds, yellows, and blues, are all about equal in abilities, granting that certain members within each group have more or less of one characteristic than another.

However, in spite of the absence of any moral-sounding words in "All men are equal," it clearly could mean something moral, since "All men are equal" might be a shorthand way of saying "All men are to be treated equally," which in turn begins to sound like "All men ought to be treated equally." Presumably the situation or the context itself is what tells us how indeed, whether as a scientist's or a moralist's claim, it is to be taken. In a situation in which a person's voting right is in question because of race, someone's saying "All men are equal" might just sensibly be interpreted as a roundabout way of saying "All men ought to be treated equally when it comes to voting." Although, then, the linguistic form utterances may take can vary so that moral sentences can, at times, take on the appearance of those a scientist might typically make, and the other way around; once one looks at the overall situation, the functions of what is said in scientific and moral contexts differ. In the former context, sentences (or claims) are used (or made) in order to *describe* and *predict*. In the latter context, sentences (or claims) are used (or made) in order to *prescribe, recommend,* and the like. Where actions and conditions are concerned, roughly speaking, the scientist describes both actions and conditions and also predicts what actions and conditions will take place and hold respectively. In contrast, the moralist prescribes and recommends actions (and conditions).

III.
GENERALIZATION AND REASON GIVING

1. Rules in moral situations

In searching for general features of moral situations, certain differences among these situations should not be overlooked. One such difference was noted in Chapter I when the distinction was made between an unproblematic moral situation and a problematic one. However, some of the sketches show the need for a further distinction among problematic situations. In some, the question is one of deciding what to do in a particular situation. What should a husband do about the promise he made to his wife to return home after the football game; or a businessman about his financial plight (Sketch 3)? Different from these situations are ones in which the moral problem itself is general. Now the problem is one of finding an answer not to how a person (or persons) should behave in a specific situation, but how he or they should behave in many situations. Given the situation, as an example, in which female to male birth ratio is three-and-one-half to one (Sketch 5), the question is: "What relationships should people have to one another?"

On the surface, the difference between these two kinds of situations seems obvious enough. Not only are general situations more complicated, but they seem to be more related to rule-making than do particular situations. One might think, in fact, that the key difference between the particular and the general situation is just the lack of necessity to formulate rules in deciding what to do in the former case. "After all," it might be argued; "all the judge in the particular moral situation need be interested in is a solution to the particular situation. Why should he bother to formulate general rules in order to accomplish what he is after? Clearly, most of us face certain serious problems once in a lifetime and our concern then is just to squeeze or slip by these problems as best we can. In contrast, a general problem is one which will recur and whose solution must be stated in the form of some rule or other."

There are indeed some differences between particular and general moral situations, but this characterization only partly and somewhat misleadingly tells what these differences are. Without a doubt, general situations are more complicated than particular ones. Dealing with a general problem is in part dealing with a whole series of specific moral problems. However, it is simply not true that in the particular situation there is no need to formulate or appeal to rules. To be sure, in the particular moral situation the judge arrives at a decision such as "I (you, we, etc.) ought to do such and such in *this* situation" so the agent or agents may act on it; whereas in the general moral situation the final judgment is in terms of "I (you, we, etc.) ought to act such and such in this *kind* of situation" so the agent or agents may act in *many* situations. Still, granting that the *final* formulation is different in the two types of situations, in *arriving* at his judgment about a particular situation the judge must unavoidably appeal to rules just as he must in the general situation.

To see why this is so and to see how the general can differ from the particular moral situation in another not so obvious way, it will be useful to trace a possible pattern of judging a particular situation. The situation in Chapter I of the amicable but unhappy couple in the process of separating (Sketch 13) will serve these purposes more than adequately. Both the husband and the wife, it will be remembered, are intelligent, sensitive, and generally informed adults who see their marriage as a mistake. Now their decision to dissolve their marriage (it matters not here whether their decision is a good one or not) is based upon certain reasons. For one, although they still respect, they no longer love one another. Another reason they cite is that they are still both young enough to remarry, while still another is that their relationship has not produced more of their kind. Yet another reason they give in favor of the separation is their basic maturity which permits each to understand why the other wants his freedom. Their separation, they believe, will result in little rancor. In addition, half-a-dozen other reasons all help lead to the same conclusion.

Of course, it is not enough to cite just any reasons to justify a (moral) decision; the reasons must be somehow relevant to the situation. Understandably, the amicable couple consider their lack of affection for each other such a relevant reason for seeking a divorce. However, if they allow this as a relevant reason in their situation, other things being equal, they can hardly blame anyone else for seeking a divorce for the same reason. In other words, in justifying one's judgment to do something through the use of reasons, even in a particular situation, a person is committed to an appeal to certain rules even though in expressing the final judgment (we ought to get a divorce) no explicit appeal to a rule is made.[1]

Too much should not be made of this point of similarity between the particular and the general moral situation. Although there is an appeal to rules in the process of justifying both types of final judgment, the difference in the nature of the final judgment (the one being general and the other particular) suggests that the appeal in the two cases may be to different ends. Notice how a society might formulate a moral (or legal) rule about divorces. It could

1. R. M. Hare, *Freedom & Reason* (New York: Oxford University Press, 1965), pp. 16–17.

say, "Divorces ought to be granted for reasons of adultery, cruelty, and non-support." What is intended here is not that all these conditions should be satisfied before a divorce would be granted, but that any one of them could bring about this effect. The conditions as listed in the rule are each sufficient to dissolve a marriage. In the case of the couple deciding on a divorce, in contrast, there is no need for them to state such sufficient conditions about divorces. Their judgment to obtain a divorce rests not on any one or even two conditions but on a peculiar combination of ten or twelve. Thus in deciding to go for a divorce, not because of reasons A or B or C or D, or . . . , but because of A *and* B *and* C *and* D, *and* . . . , taken together, their situation may be so unique as to tempt them not to universalize or generalize their result. Yet, however unlikely it might be, if another couple under circumstances A and B and C and D and . . . desire a divorce, the first couple would have to make their own final decision applicable to this couple as well. In this sense their specific judgment is also a rule—in disguise as it were. However, it is a rule with so many qualifications that it may not be usable as a rule. So even though a moral decision (whether general or particular) is justified by an appeal to at least one rule, and the final (particular) decision is generalizable in principle, this latter decision need not necessarily come to be used or treated as a rule.

2. *The functions of rules*

All this raises the question of how rules are used and also how they can be misused under certain circumstances. A rule certainly is used as a guide for conduct, and as a guide it must help lead or direct our behavior. We speak of an agent as following a rule. Presumably, in part what this means is that he is aware of the rule *and* is trying to act in accordance with it. The awareness is evidently important here, otherwise we would speak of him as not *following* but merely *acting in accordance with* the rules (perhaps by accident, unconsciously, or by habit). But if moral rules are meant to be followed (consciously) they must be stated simply in order to be easily understood and applied. After all, moral rules are intended to be followed by ordinary people as well as by technicians and scholars. To state a rule, therefore, with so many qualifications that it becomes difficult to understand and apply is in effect not to state a rule at all, but to make a specific moral judgment instead. Further, as a rule becomes increasingly qualified it becomes increasingly degeneralized and thus loses its guidance power. If a judgment in a moral situation becomes extremely complicated because of appeals to many reasons or rules, as with the amicable couple, similar complicated situations had best be looked at individually, since they may, and probably do, differ in subtle and significant ways from the original situation. In short, the original complicated situation probably cannot be used as a model for handling similar situations.

The time-saving aspect of rules in moral situations can now be better appreciated. An appeal to previous decisions which can be taken as rules (at least of one type) is primarily useful in what might be called standard situations —those which are not complicated and not unique. To be sure, even in so-called standard moral situations an appeal to the facts of the case is always in order. Even if we suppose that beating one's wife is not a practice to be encouraged, the fact of the beating must still be established before the husband can be said to be guilty. Still, having rules only so that the facts of the case need to be established in order to render a judgment saves time by literally enabling people to carry on their lives. For if each moral situation had to be decided upon not only as to the facts of the case but also as to the moral rules behind the decision, many decisions simply would not be made. The extra time involved in dealing with each moral situation would be comparable to taking every legal case all the way to the Supreme Court. Appealing to moral rules, then, is necessary not only logically, since moral judgments are made by appeals to (descriptive) reasons[2] and these appeals presuppose appeals to rules, but also practically, since the judge in moral situations would simply not get his job done if he could not appeal to his past judgments as expressed in rules.

Moral rules have still other functions. Up to now these rules have been spoken of mainly with respect to the person playing the judge's and the agent's roles. For the judge, rules are needed in order to formulate judgments and other rules. Rules are also time savers. For the agents, rules guide his behavior. But rules are just as important for the patient and others involved in moral situations, such as friends of the patient. When the agent announces that such and such a rule will guide his behavior, others now know what to expect from him. In this sense, rules and the following of rules help to organize life. Rules act as plans enabling one human being to know what to expect from another.

3. Dangers in the use of rules

For all their value, the various uses of rules in moral situations are not without their dangers. One important danger has already been alluded to. In non-standard situations in which many new or hard to uncover (e.g., psychological) factors are present, a rethinking of the whole situation is advisable. But the very time-saving advantage of appealing to rules may tempt someone not to review a situation in need of review. Other personal reasons may also tempt one not to initiate a general review. It may be both comforting and profitable, for example, for a real estate agent to want the laws and moral rules, however outdated and unfair they might be, to be applied severely against the "criminal element" which is sponsoring some "civil rights" disturbance. Such an appeal to rules, used perhaps less as a way of guiding behavior and more as a

2. *Ibid.*, pp. 16–17.

way of placing it on rigid tracks, would have to be guarded against.

On the other hand, the opposite move of treating each case as unique and unconventional also has its pitfalls. In an admittedly exaggerated manner, the two opposing dangers can be characterized as follows: By rigidly appealing to rules, the Conservative standardizes all moral situations and thereby limits moral thinking. For him, certain aspects of moral thinking are unnecessary. All he demands is the correct application of rules already accepted with whatever already accepted exceptions may be built into them. No new rules and no new exceptions to these rules are permitted and, in this sense, no new moral problems need to be anticipated. For the Liberal, all situations are exceptions and therefore all moral situations are problematic situations. But the price the Liberal pays for all his moral problems is too high. By making every situation an exception, he destroys moral rules. For if there were a rule which supposedly is to guide the behavior of a classroom, but each student in the class is somehow able to make himself exempt from following the rule because he thinks *his* situation is different, the rule is a rule in name only. More importantly, not only does the Liberal destroy the old rules of "reaction" by claiming that each moral situation is unique, he also makes it impossible for himself, again because of the uniqueness of each situation, to devise new "liberal" rules. So both positions lead to difficulties if not absurdities.

The third danger may be more serious than the first two, since cases of it are more difficult to identify. The reason for this difficulty is the apparent reasonableness of persons who succumb to this danger. Aware that they are expected to justify any claim they make about a moral situation, people satisfy this expectation by offering a reason which indeed backs the claim. And that is just the danger. By giving one, or at best two or three reasons, the impression is left that the judgment has been justified and the judge involved has been reasonable, since he can now say, "We ought to do X *because* of Y." But such a person has not necessarily been reasonable, for in dealing with moral problems it is not enough to give *a* reason or even *several reasons* to back up a judgment. One must give all the relevant known or obtainable reasons. When one says, "We ought to do X because of Y," stops and then says no more, he implies that there are no other (known) reasons.

There is another possibility here and it leads to a fourth danger in the use of rules in moral situations. In saying "We (I, you) ought to do X because of Y," the judge in this situation may not actually imply that there are no other reasons, but that there are no other *important* reasons. Not only then is giving *a* or *a series* of reasons not enough, it is not enough in order to be reasonable just to give all the known or obtainable reasons in serial order. What more is needed evidently is some sort of ranking or ordering of the reasons, for some may not only be more important than others but some may overlap, be subsumed by, or even conflict with others.

4. The role of value judgments

As a result of these dangers, the process of reason-giving begins to look increasingly difficult to apply. Actually, there are even more difficulties or at least complications involved here. What has been said thus far about dealing with problematic moral situations is:

1. The final judgment made is generalizable to similar situations, although when highly qualified the generalized judgment can be thought of as a rule in principle only and not in practice;

2. The final judgment is justified by reasons which seem to presuppose the existence of a rule or rules other than the final judgment (generalized).

Now it is in this second area, of justifying a final judgment, in contrast to merely uttering or making a final judgment, in which the complications enter in. These complications pertain to the sorts of reasons which can be used to justify a final judgment. Basically there are three types. To say "You ought to do X because he hit you (he no longer loves you, he is your father, you are a citizen, or God loves you)" is to give *factual* or what might more generally be termed *descriptive* reasons to back up a moral judgment. Such reasons give information about what is or what is believed to be the case. Although these reasons are an important and perhaps a necessary part of the process of seeking solutions to moral problems, they can hardly be the whole story; for one can say of any such reason given as justification for a judgment: "So what? So he hit you! (So God loves you?, etc.)" Now it may be obvious that because someone hit you (not in a prize fight but in the street in such a way as to embarrass and hurt you) you ought to do something about it. However, what makes it obvious is not *just* the fact that you were hit. Nor is the fact that you were hurt normally thought of as enough of a reason to completely back up your judgment that you ought to retaliate or turn the other cheek. In some cases what more is needed is some *moral rule* to show how the situation, being hit, requires a certain sort of action such as retaliation. The rule in cases like these performs the function of claiming the situation to be a normal one and thus to be handled in accordance with the rule. To cite a rule then, in this context, is like saying that what just happened has happened before, and we agreed in the past that it should be handled in the following way. So in addition to citing *facts* to back moral judgments, *moral rules,* at least on some occasions, can also be used to back these judgments. Further, as was noted earlier, when so used, moral rules show the *relevance* of the fact to the situation. It is because there is a rule about hitting someone and turning the other cheek that mention of the hitting is relevant to the moral situation.

There is no question but that in dealing with some moral problems it is enough to cite facts to settle them. Often one has only to cite facts because those to whom the justification is being presented already agree with you about the rules.[3] What they want to be apprised of are the facts so that they may know which rules to apply. At other times, when the rules are forgotten, their appropriateness is not clear, or when one or more of several rules may be applicable, a moral question may not be settled until some appeal to rules is made. Still and all, although some, or most, moral questions may be settled on one of these two levels, a third kind of appeal may be needed in an attempt to clean up the remainder. This appeal can be thought of as one to higher moral rules, perhaps ones high enough to be called moral principles. Yet this would be somewhat misleading, since some of these so-called rules or principles are not really rules or principles as such. Rules guide action or conduct. They tell us to keep promises, tell the truth, help our neighbors when they are in distress, or what have you. But if instead of saying "You ought to tell the truth" and thus express a rule of conduct, one says "Pleasure (physical) is a good," he seems to be expressing a general judgment of a sort which is not a rule itself. Nor is it easily reducible to a rule. It might seem otherwise, for to say "Physical pleasure is a good" might be thought of as another way of expressing the rule "You ought to seek pleasure (physical)." But the trouble here is that "You ought to seek physical pleasure" does not really prescribe conduct.[4] The word "seek", or others which might be used here to do a similar job such as "reach for" or "strive for," suggest not that some conduct has been found and is being prescribed but, just the opposite, that this conduct must be found. What a sentence such as "Seek physical pleasure" or "Pleasure is a good" does is help establish what *values* or *goals* persons should hold—not specifically what conduct they should employ in order to hold or reach these values.

---

3. Charles L. Stevenson, *Ethics and Language* (New Haven: Yale University Press, 1944), pp. 2–19. See especially Professor Stevenson's discussion of disagreement in beliefs.

4. There is more trouble here too, for to say that something is good (or a good) does not imply that it ought to be sought necessarily, for there may be "better goods."

Putting it in this way shows how these *value judgments* can be tied in with moral rules, just as moral rules are tied in with factual reasons. In some circumstances when justification for a moral judgment is being given, factual reason giving leads to rule reason giving. "I ought to help him because he helped me" leads to "One ought always to return friendly favors, etc. . . ." But just as the question "So what?" may be asked in response to factual reason giving in a moral situation, so the question "Why?" or some similar question may be asked in response to rule citing. And although it seems likely that some rules can be justified in terms of an appeal to other rules, it is difficult to imagine what sense such appeals could make unless they rest on some value judgment. It is not as if (conduct) rules are good in and of themselves. Telling the truth, considered as a type of action, has no value in and of itself. If I, as the sole source of information, fail to tell the "truth" to a computer or even to a community of computers, I may very well disorganize each and every one of them. Yet "What of it?" someone may ask. Unless the object or some aspect of the object were valued in and of itself, it would really not matter what we "said" to the computers, "truths" or "lies." But if we are lying to humans instead, it seems to make a difference. Perhaps it makes a difference because humans have feelings, are worthy of attention, or are to be valued for their own sake.[5]

Problematic moral situations may involve still more steps in reason giving. For now, however, it seems clear that there are these three levels of reasoning in dealing with a moral problem: the factual or descriptive level, the rule, and the value level. Actually, some doubt has been

5. "It is generally agreed among those who have thought on the subject that, with the possible exception of beautiful objects, valuable on account of their beauty, a merely physical thing cannot be good in itself but only good as a means. Apart at least from the very doubtful exception just mentioned, what is good in itself must be an experience, state of mind or life, it cannot be anything without consciousness at all." A. C. Ewing, *Ethics* (London: English Universities Press Ltd., 1953), p. 7.

raised recently as to whether making value judgments or commitments in the sense discussed here is strictly speaking a part of moral reasoning.[6] Some analysts of moral situations prefer not to think of value judgments as a part of moral situations. One reason for thinking along these lines is the already observed point that value judgments do not directly prescribe actions. But, according to this view, when we speak of moral rules and principles and the moral point of view, this is just what we think of. It is not that value judgments do not enter into moral situations, but that their role in these situations is one of *non*-moral judgments being employed in moral situations. This is actually the main, and second, argument of this position. Value judgments are not really moral judgments in the strict sense, since they can be used not only in moral situations but in personal or prudential ones as well. This, of course, is not to say they are immoral, but rather that they can better be spoken of as non-moral. They are like a housekeeper who works in a home, and other homes as well, but does not live in or belong to any one of these homes. Thus, on this view, we can say "Seek pleasure" or "Pleasure is the highest goal" and plug these value judgments into our moral reasoning, *or* into our reasoning which might be aimed at convincing someone of something about how to run his personal affairs, but strictly speaking when we do these things we are not reasoning morally or "personally."

Although in one sense this issue of the status of value judgments is interesting, it may be beside the point. As long as value judgments of some sort or other are found in moral situations—implicitly or explicitly—it would be proper to point to them and show what functions they play in moral situations as a part of the answer to the most general question of this work, What is a moral situation? In a similar sense, factual reasons can be thought of as external or

6. William K. Frankena, *Ethics* (Englewood Cliffs, N.J.: 1963), pp. 8–10, 47–48.

"extra-moral" reasons used in moral situations, since they play roles in scientific situations also. Yet it has been found to be important to analyze the roles these reasons play in moral situations in order to understand the overall nature of moral situations. Nevertheless, there are some reasons to suppose that value judgments so called are not just *found* in moral situations or even are not just necessary non-moral elements in moral situations. One reason is suggested by the sketch of the magazine publisher who quite openly and honestly believes in and preaches on behalf of the pleasures of the body (Sketch 9). He is not only honest, but he never breaks promises or commits crimes. Nor does he perform any wrong action covered under what would be considered an accepted moral rule except as it might interfere with the achievement of his main goals. Similarly, in his preachings he argues strongly for honesty and other moral rules in achieving what he considers to be man's highest goals. Yet in spite of his wide agreement with the public on what moral rules to follow, he is thought of by many people as being thoroughly immoral. Why? Because of the different moral *rules* he advocates? To be sure, in spite of his general agreement with the public on many moral rules, he and his followers do have their own special rules such as "Concealth not the beauty of the body" and "Acquaintance with the body pleasures as early in adult life as possible is desirable." Still, since these rules are so patently connected with his basic value judgments, it seems strained to call him immoral because of the rules but not because of his value judgments or principles. One's value judgments or principles, insofar as they set goals, cannot help in some sense also to set the moral rules.

A second reason indicating why value judgments are indeed a part of moral situations in the broad sense conceived in this work is the use of the word "principle" in connection with talk about values. Principles as well as rules are part and parcel of our talk about moral situations. We speak not only of *following* moral rules but also of *holding* onto moral principles. The difference in how we talk about these two concepts is significant. A rule is spoken of as being followed insofar as it serves to guide our behavior along a path, as it were. As was noted earlier, we can also speak of acting in accordance with a rule. Both "following" and "acting in accordance with" are appropriate to rules, since moral rules literally tell us *what* to do. But a principle may be something else again. At times a principle does as a matter of fact guide our behavior, since principles are sometimes thought of as very general rules, as "Love thy neighbor" (not in the magazine publisher's sense) might be, for example. But principles need not always be thought of as rules in the sense of literally guiding behavior. This is part of the force of saying that we cling to, hold to, keep our eye on, or commit ourselves to principles, rather than follow them. The principle which we cling to is often the value judgment which is the goal the individual sets for himself or society. It makes sense to cling to such a principle, since as a goal one must constantly "set one's eyes on it" and resist the pressures of daily life in order to reach it. Thus to the extent that we speak of moral principles and these principles are not literally rules of action, but value judgments instead, it again seems strange to think of these judgments as merely outsiders found in moral situations rather than intrinsic parts of moral situations.

There is still another reason, a more fundamental one, why value judgments are not just outsiders, like housekeepers, who do some work in moral situations from time to time, or even on a regular basis. This reason has to do with a comparison of the roles factual reasons, so-called moral rules proper, and value judgments play in moral situations. Those who think of value judgments as outsiders with respect to moral situations compare these judgments with factual judgments or reasons which are also thought of as outsiders. Just as a factual reason, so the argument goes, can be used in scientific, prudential situations as well as moral situations, so also can value judgments be used in situations *other* than moral ones. The assumption here is that, in contrast to the outsider, a true insider in a moral situation would be used only in moral situations. Candidates for insiders, for those aspects of a moral situation which are intrinsically and uniquely moral, are the so-called moral rules. But what are these rules? Presumably they are rules like "Don't kill" and "Keep promises." The trouble here, however, is that although these rules sound moral enough to do the job, they themselves no more satisfy the conditions for a true insider than value judgments do, since one can always keep a promise for prudential reasons (in prudential situations) in addition to moral ones. One can also keep from killing for prudential reasons (in prudential situations) as well as moral ones. And so on. Of course, one could argue that "Don't kill" or "You ought to keep a promise" have what might be called their strictly "moral senses." But this merely shows that these claims have other senses than the moral and therefore are not themselves uniquely and intrinsically moral in the required sense. The point is then that if a value judgment is not an intrinsic part of the moral situation because it does outside work, a so-called moral rule is equally non-intrinsic because it also does outside work.

This conclusion turns "What makes a moral situation moral?" a species of the "What is a moral situation?" question, into a baffling sort of question. One wants to say that what makes a moral situation moral must be some element in the situation, whatever it might be, which itself is uniquely moral. Like a human who is said by some to be human because he possesses a unique human soul, so a situation is supposed to be moral because it has some unique moral component (e.g., some quality, relation, rule) in it. But when we look for the alleged moral component and fail to find its "moral-ness" we are puzzled. We think perhaps we ought to look harder. And perhaps we should. We also perhaps ought to look at the model we are using to answer the question "What makes a moral situation moral?" A moral situation may be less like a human with a soul and more like, say, a lion. A lion is not normally thought of as a lion because it has lion parts, but the other way around; the parts are labelled lion parts because they are parts of a lion. Similarly it may be that a moral situation is not moral because of any *one* of its parts (e.g., rules) but because of the way the parts are put together as a whole. Thus the rule (or value judgment) cited in a moral situation may not be what makes the situation a moral one. Rather, the rule (or value judgment) cited may be treated as a moral rule (or value judgment) because it is cited in a moral situation. If the situation makes the rules and other parts of a situation moral and not the other way around, the task of the philosopher is not to look for the one moral "quality" or whatever, but rather to characterize those combinations of circumstances or aspects which make a situation a moral one. And this is just what this study is about. Just as the lion is composed of a series of parts no one of which is labelled "lion," so moral situations may best be thought of as having such "parts" as agents, actions, rules, patients, conditions, and value judgments—no one of which can be labelled intrinsically moral.

IV.
PERSONAL, SELF-INTEREST, SOCIAL, AND MORAL SITUATIONS

1. Strictly personal and moral situations

Having seen how the concepts of agent, patient, judge, rule, and principle (among others) are directly tied in with understanding the more general concept of the moral situation, it is useful now to take an indirect view of some different aspects of moral situations by contrasting other practical and value situations to moral ones. One of the problems in effecting such a contrast is in deciding how to classify some of these various non-moral situations. Should, for example, political (or legal) situations be classed under the category of social situations, or are they different enough to deserve separate treatment?[1] And when a person speaks of a political (or legal) situation as not being a moral one, as he does when he says, "This is a political matter, not a moral one," does he really mean what it sounds as if he is saying—that moral rules, reasons, and the rest simply do not apply here? If he means that these non-moral situations do indeed have nothing to do with morality, then the overall picture of moral among other principles and value situations which he is drawing will be one in which the moral realm constitutes just one aspect of our life among

---

1. This is a question which time will prevent answering here.

others, and perhaps only one small aspect of our life at that. In the process of contrasting moral with non-moral situations I will argue that this picture is misleading, for moral situations do have a special status over many (and perhaps all) other practical and value situations. In this sense they do not form just another but *the* most important aspect of our (value) life.

Among the many non-moral situations which resemble moral ones enough to cause some confusion are so-called personal ones. When one thinks of what to eat, wear, the style of home to buy, the kind of work he will engage in, when he will get out of bed on his day off, the color of car he likes, the type of music he prefers—all of these things and more can be characterized as personal or even *strictly* personal. What is normally involved in making decisions of this type, in picking out a color for a car one can afford, for example, is simply deciding what one likes. Puzzlement in situations like these is indeed often expressed in terms of "Oh what *do* I want?" The question is not, in other words, whether to act as one wants. That decision, presumably, has already been made. Rather the question is to come to a decision about what one wants now (regardless of the future) or about what one may likely want over a period of time. Especially in the latter case, the question is one of gaining self-knowlege so as to act in a way to please oneself. Typically, in these personal situations then, the agent, patient, and judge are one and the same person, although sometimes others may help us to assess what it is we like and how to attain it.

Yet it is not enough in characterizing personal situations merely to note that they are of, by, and for the person involved; for someone might consider torturing others to be one of the little pleasures of life. If he were to do so, we would probably remind him that no matter how much he enjoys such activity the situation is not a personal one any longer but has become an interpersonal one instead. With this reminder, the contrast between personal and moral situations begins to become evident. In *part* this contrast is built upon the difference between "me" and "other-than-me." When others are involved (especially as patients) in some action I perform, I can no longer consider the situation to be strictly personal. In fact, when pressed about a decision which I claim to be strictly personal, I must be prepared to prove that it is not interpersonal. If someone proves my so-called "strictly personal" actions to have significant effects upon others, I am refuted not because the reasons I have given for personally making the choice are wrong, but because I have given the wrong *kind* of reason. If the claim of some analysts about moral situations is true—that these situations are interpersonal (or social) in nature[2]—then the point about a moral situation not being just one of many other types of practical and/or value situations becomes partly understandable. It is not as if a person has a choice of operating on the personal or interpersonal (moral) level so that he can say "Well, your values are on the moral level, but I personally prefer the personal myself" and thereby absolve himself of moral responsibilities. Rather one cannot be said to be in a personal situation unless he can show first that this situation does not have moral implications. If it does, it becomes a moral

2. Baier says in his *The Moral Point of View (op. cit.)*: "It will be obvious from the position I have taken elsewhere that in my view morality arises out of the relations between individuals, that there would be no need for and no point in having a morality if people had no sort of contact with others, that the solitary individual could employ his reason in practical matters only from the point of view of self interest, never from the moral point of view. If individuals live by themselves and cannot affect one another, then, morally speaking, there is nothing they may not do or refrain from doing. A world of Robinson Crusoes has no need for a morality and no use for one. Moral distinctions do not apply to it." p. 215. Similarly Singer says in *Generalization in Ethics (op. cit.)*: "In saying that a vice is an undesirable trait or habit, we must distinguish the interests with respect to which it is undesirable, the person or group of persons *for whom* it is undesirable. If it is harmful to the person who has it, then it is undesirable with respect to his interests, and then it is undesirable from the point of prudence. It is, consequently, a self-regarding, inprudential vice. On the other hand, if it is harmful to another or to society, then it is undesirable with respect to their interests and is thus morally undesirable." p. 318.

situation instead of a strictly personal one. Not only, then, do the two types of situations exclude one another (i.e., one cannot be in both a personal and a moral situation) but, in a sense, moral situations have priority over the personal ones.

2. Personal and prudential situations

In view of this priority it is interesting to seek a contrast not only between personal and moral, but between prudential and moral situations as well. But in order to do this, a further contrast needs to be made between personal and prudential situations. On the surface both of these types of situations would seem to be alike. They both refer to the individual insofar as thinking about these situations is always in terms of "for me." But a difference appears in the way in which they refer to the individual. Personal situations were just now characterized in terms of such little pleasures of life as car colors, types of food, drink, and clothes. In speaking of prudential matters, however, it seems hardly appropriate to talk of the little pleasures of life. Rather we are concerned with such things as life insurance, an education, taking care in crossing the street, or paying the mobsters "protection money." Whereas a (strictly) personal situation seems to deal more with what we like or gives us pleasure, a prudential one deals with what is good for us.

As was mentioned already, although at times we may need help from others in gaining self-knowledge about our likes and pleasures, by and large it is we who are in the best position to know about them. This is less likely to be the case with questions of prudence or, as they are sometimes called, questions of self-interest. At certain stages and under certain conditions in our lives, such as when we are very young, intoxicated, emotionally disturbed, fatigued, sick, or in a new situation, we might very well have little conception of what is in our interest. More than that, what is in our interest may involve activities and experiences from which we simply obtain no pleasure at all (such as going to the dentist). So although acting in one's self-interest involves the agent treating himself as the patient, it does not necessarily involve the agent as also being the judge in the situation. In contrast, in personal situations the agent, patient, and judge are typically all the same. In this sense, personal situations—especially those sometimes called strictly personal—are indeed just that.

Granting the above differences between personal and self-interest situations, how do the two relate to one another? Do they, as with moral and personal situations, exclude one another? Imagine the following not uncommon type of situation. John smokes cigarettes and has done so for several years. Along with smoking he enjoys reading, watching sports programs on TV, painting, listening to music on his hi-fi set, tennis, and his bachelor existence. But now his tennis partner, a medical man, notices that John's game is off and that recently John rarely wins the third and usually decisive set in their bi-weekly match. He advises John to give up smoking, as he says, "For your own good." Given the fact that John's smoking is affecting his health, is the situation still to be characterized as a (strictly) personal one? In one sense it seems as if it still can be, for he has been advised, not commanded or forced, to give up cigarettes; and thus the choice is still his. Further, whatever he does, whether he continues smoking and enjoying cigarettes or mends his ways, it is his own personal pleasure and interest which are at stake. Yet in another sense the doctor's revelation of the damage cigarette smoking is doing to John's health has changed the situation. The doctor might have put it as follows: "This is no longer *just* a matter of what you like." To be sure, the pleasure John receives from smoking is still a consideration, but it is no longer the sole or even the major consideration. Since it is not, and since John presumably wants to live and is interested in his own welfare, the situation or problem is no longer a strictly personal one. Thus, the reasons he gives for and against smoking cigarettes cannot be expressed just in terms of his likes (the taste, inhaling,

etc.) and dislikes (the occasional dried-out feeling he gets
when he oversmokes) but rather in terms of what is good
for him.[3] John himself in his weakness, assuming for the
moment that he finds it difficult to give up smoking, might
express the situation as follows and reflect at the same time
the change which has taken place. He might say, "I know I
shouldn't smoke but I can't help it. I can't quit! I enjoy
smoking too much." The argument is that for John to talk
this way is for him and his doctor to realize how the self-
interest situation has replaced the one I have been calling a
strictly personal one. The two do seem to exclude one another much as the moral and personal do.

3. Self-interest and moral situations

Complicating John's plight will serve to raise the question of whether self-interest and moral situations exclude
one another as well. Assume now that John has not given
up smoking but he has given up his bachelor existence.
Not only that, but with the passage of time he finds himself happily burdened with the responsibilities of raising
children. While all this is going on, his health continues to
deteriorate mainly because of his heavy smoking. His doctor friend now has a new argument. "It is not any longer,"
he says, "just a matter of something you like or even of self-
interest. Even if you don't care about yourself, for the sake
of your family you have a moral duty to give up smoking."

Whatever it is that has turned the situation into a moral
one—and it is temptingly wrong to say that the situation is
a moral one *simply* because it is *other* rather than *self*
oriented[4]—what the doctor says does suggest the exclusion

---

3. It may be still possible to speak of John as being in two situations
(prudential and strictly personal) rather than one situation (prudential). In other words, it may be that John faces a strictly personal
problem (concerned with the little pleasures and pains of life) and a
prudential one (his health). However, I think we are more likely to
treat it as one and allow the more important (the prudential) to
encompass the less important. More on the concept of encompassing
later in this chapter.

4. In effect this is what Baier and Singer are saying in footnote 2.

of the self-interest situation by the moral one. Just as with John's discovery of the ill effect smoking has on his health, John cannot say that he still considers the situation a strictly personal one (of the pleasure he gets from smoking). He cannot say this, because for him to show that it is strictly personal is for him not only to like smoking but to show that nothing else (e.g., self-interest) is involved. Similarly, for someone to be in a self-interest situation is for him not only to act in his self-interest, if he is so inclined, but to be able to show that no one else's interest is involved.

At this point a distinction should be made in order to avoid confusion. There is a difference between *an appeal* to one's self-interest and a self-interest *situation*. The latter is what I have been arguing is excluded by a moral situation. Situations exclude one another, not appeals. Clearly, in trying to convince someone to do something which he morally should do, I can appeal to moral grounds, but failing that, try to appeal to his self-interest if indeed this person's self-interest is also at stake. I might even appeal to what he likes in the sense of appealing to reasons which are strictly personal. I might do all this quite obviously, because although he is in a moral situation he may not recognize that he is, and even if he does, he may not be moved to act on such a basis. Thus, although we may appeal to one's self-interest in order to get him to act in a moral situation, this does not necessarily mean that he is in a self-interest situation.

Considering the status of the three types of situations discussed up to this point, they do appear to exclude one another. In dealing with a problem, it cannot be classified as a personal, self-interest, *and* a moral problem—if in fact it is not some other type of problem altogether. More than that, however, the manner in which these types of problems exclude one another suggests a hierarchy of exclusion. Since for a problem to be classifiable as a strictly personal one, reasons of self-interest and morality must be shown not to apply; such problems are on the low end of the totem pole. They are excluded when it can be shown that a problem which was thought to be a strictly personal one has some self-interest or moral aspects to it. Similarly, a situation which involves someone's self-interest, but which has moral ramifications to it, cannot be considered to be a self-interest situation. So moral reasons override self-interest and, of course, strictly personal ones as well. The contrast of moral to these other two types of situation is, as was claimed earlier, not of one type of value situation which is merely different from the other type, all on the same level as it were, but of three different types of situations on three different levels.

4. Self-obligations

A related point of contrast between moral, on the one side, and strictly personal and self-interest situations, on the other, has been alluded to already. In the case of John the Smoker, self-interest (and strictly personal) matters seemed to yield to moral ones with the introduction of others—in this case with the introduction of a wife and children into his life. Situations like these, and other considerations, have led some analysts of moral situations to conclude that duties, obligations, and the like pertain only to others and not to oneself.[5] These analysts admit that in some indirect sense one may have an obligation to oneself. Thus John might morally say things like "I promised myself to give up smoking" or even "I have a duty to myself to do so." But, according to this account, it makes sense morally for John to carry out such a duty not really because of himself but because of his family. Strictly speaking, according to this view, if John did not have a family and could not do things for himself which *in turn* benefit his family or which are based on promises made to them, but still said "I have a duty to myself," he would merely be talking non-morally about his self-interest, or speaking emphatically, or perhaps speaking misleadingly.

5. Baier, *op. cit.*, pp. 214–230; Singer, *op. cit.*, pp. 311–318.

One reason this interpretation of the contrast of moral and self-interest situations sounds plausible is the way self-interest and strictly personal considerations often seem to be opposed to moral ones. Going to war for the sake of one's country tends to block, and sometimes block totally, one's personal pleasures and self-interest. So also can one's pleasures and interests be blocked by other community obligations (such as jury service) and family obligations. There is, therefore, no question but that one's self-interests and moral obligations are often opposed to one another. Yet they also often coincide. If John had given up smoking for his family's sake, he would also have been serving his self-interest (but not necessarily his strictly personal pleasures) even though he is not in a self-interest situation once he gains a wife and children. There are cases even when one's moral duties, self-interest, and little pleasures all coincide, as they would if John were to improve himself by studying for an advanced academic degree in a field which he likes and in which obtaining the degree also serves to better support his family. But still, when duty and self-interest coincide they would appear to be *just* coinciding. And insofar as they just coincide as a matter of fact, the possibility of a fundamental opposition of self-interest and the little pleasures of life with morality would always seem to be there.

Although one's duties may, and often do, "fall out" with his little pleasures and self-interest, something more than coincidence tends to bring them back together again. Self-interest and the little pleasures of life are not opposed, or more accurately are not irrelevant, to morality, as may be implied by the view which says that we cannot have obligations to ourselves. One's self-interests (again not to be confused with self-interest situations) are not excluded by morality, but rather *can* be a part of it. Some explanation of this point is in order.

Much of the previous chapter was concerned with exploring the sense in which the moral obligations are rule-following situations. But a rule-following situation is one in which something general can be said or implied. Toulmin put it this way:

> As ethical judgements become more general, specific references to 'me,' 'here' and 'now,' 'them' 'there' and 'then' are eliminated, and as long as any such references remain, there is room for an appeal to a more general principle. The point at which the justification of a moral decision must cease is where the action under discussion has been unambiguously related to a current 'moral principle,' independent (in its wording) of person, place and time: e.g. where 'I ought to take this book and give it back to Jones at once' has given way to 'Anyone ought always to do anything that he promises anyone else that he will do' or 'It was a promise.' If, in justifying an action, we can carry our reasons back to such universal principles, our justification has some claim to be called 'ethical.' But, if we cannot do so, our appeal is not to 'morality' at all: if, for example, the most general principles to which we can appeal still contain some reference to us, either as individuals or as members of a limited group of people, then our appeal is not to 'morality' but to 'privilege.'[6]

On first reading, Toulmin might be taken to be arguing for a direct conflict of duty and interest. This is not so. He is not saying that my (self) interests cannot count morally, but rather that these interests cannot be given privileged status. For that matter, no persons's interests can be given privileged status. When my interests are given such status, when "the most general principles to which we can appeal still contain some reference to" me, what I am in effect doing is turning a moral situation into a self-interest one. This has to be a mistake, for I know I am in a moral situation but justify my actions by means of a self-interest argument, I imply that the situation is of the self-interest type. But to do this is in effect to deny that I am in a moral situation. The reason for this is that, as was already argued, a self-interest *situation* is one which takes one's interests into ac-

6. S. E. Toulmin, *The Place of Reason in Ethics, op. cit.* p. 168.

count *and* implies that no one else's interests are involved. To the extent then that the interests of people pertain to moral situations, each and every one's interests must at least be *considered*. In such a family moral situation as John finds himself, in which each member counts as a human being, John's pleasures and welfare are as important as anyone else's. Morally his interests are being taken account of, but being taken account of in proper perspective as one member of a human family. Of course, under certain circumstances his interests may count less or actually more than those of the other members of his family. But they will count more or less *not* because they are *his*. That would be treating a moral situation as if it were a self-interest one once again. Rather his interests will count more or less because of certain reasons such as age, health, his position as father in the family, or because of what he has promised.

In effect this means that moral situations have an *encompassing* feature in that they encompass or take in factors from situations which they override. Thus in situations which have moral implications, consideration is given to the interests (desires or whatever) of others, but not exclusively so, for consideration must be given to my (your) interests as well. It is not then just coincidence, as was suggested earlier, that my interests may very well tend to correspond to what is morally right. At times, under certain circumstances, I may actually be obligated to look after my own interests just as much as I might look after the interests of others under different circumstances. Again, when I morally look after my interests, I must do so with a reason other than "Well, after all, they are *my* interests!" I must do so with reasons such as "My interests in going to college and receiving this scholarship should receive preference over yours because my academic achievements are greater than yours and scholarships should be awarded on the basis of academic achievement." In short, morality possesses this encompassing feature because everyone, not just others, you, or I, can receive consideration. *No one* need be excluded.

The encompassing feature of a moral situation, more particularly the judgments about these situations, can be appreciated even more by another argument. If moral judgments to be moral must be based upon completely general principles, as some modern writers have been saying, with no reference to time, place, or person as such, then moral judgments cannot be just about others, since "others" is *not* itself a completely general word. It can only be understood in terms of some reference to the speaker or someone else. What it means is "other than *me (you)*" or simply "not *me (you)*." If someone, then, in opposing morality to self-interest, claims that whenever we act morally our own interests must not be considered in and of themselves, but only as a means to helping others (such as one's family), he has to be wrong, because a truly general moral principle cannot be stated with such disguised pronouns as "others" implied in the statement of the principle.

Lest there be misunderstanding of what is being said here, certain points ought to be reiterated and summarized. First, since they exclude one another, moral and self-interest *situations* cannot (although moral and self-interest appeals can) conflict with one another. They exclude one another simply because a self-interest situation is, in part, one which has no moral ramifications.[7] I cannot claim that what I do on vacation is (just) a matter of self-interest when, for example, certain moral considerations such as the welfare of my family are also at stake. Second, although when I am in a self-interest situation there *cannot* be moral ramifications, when I am in a moral situation

7. In a somewhat similar sense self-interest (or prudential) situations probably encompass what I have been calling strictly personal ones. The difference seems to be that when the self-interest encompasses (includes the factors of the) strictly personal situation it apparently *treats* the two distinct situations *as if* they were one. The little pleasures which make up the strictly personal situation do not literally become factors which make up one's self-interest after all. When the moral encompasses the self-interest and the strictly personal situations, in contrast, it seems to *make* two (or three) situations into one. The reason for this is that one's own interests literally become a part of the moral situation along with everyone else's.

there *can* be self-interest ramifications. This is so because, although moral situations exclude self-interest situations, they can encompass or include my interests along with everyone else's. Three, to say that my interests are included in moral assessments (of moral situations) is only to say that they will receive consideration. My interests, therefore, will *not necessarily* count as much as others', but these interests will be weighed *along with* others' interests on the basis of some principle (e.g., of humanity, usefulness, etc.). Saying all this is compatible with saying that although my interests may be weighed, the weight assigned on moral grounds to them may (unfortunately for me) turn out to be zero.

Two things follow from the above three points. First, from point one about how moral and self-interest situations cannot conflict it follows that when one is in a situation he must first ask himself whether it has moral ramifications. Someone, call him Charlie (Sketch 10), who thinks only about himself and measures all things and people (including family, friends, etc.) in terms of his own interests, is treating all situations as if they were self-interest ones. Yet because he has not even asked any moral questions, he is in no position to know if and when he is in situations of self-interest, since again, in order to know whether he is in such situations, he must first exclude the possibility that he is in any moral situation. From the fact that Charlie has never thought morally it does not necessarily follow that his actions are immoral; for, among other things, his self-interests may coincide with what is morally correct. Nevertheless, when compared with someone who at least occasionally thinks on moral grounds, this person's actions probably will be more in line with what is morally right than Charlie's. Thinking about one's self-interests exclusively involves one, then, not only in making the logical mistakes of not understanding what self-interest and moral situations are but also, very likely, in making moral mistakes as well.

Secondly, from points two and three above, about the

encompassing feature of morality and the considerations it gives to one's interests respectively, the possibility of obligations to oneself follows. One reason we are hesitant to admit this possibility has to do with psychology. If people have obligations to themselves and to others, psychologically they seem strangely better able to recognize and act on the former obligations than on the latter. In principle, however, there is no reason why a person—call him Albert—should not act morally not only to favor his interests but also to prefer his interests to others. In doing so, of course, Albert must act on some principle. But so long as he does he cannot be accused of acting selfishly in the sense of not thinking morally. So long as he considers others and himself, as Charlie above has not, he need not necessarily be ashamed, embarrassed, or feel guilty about acting in his own interests—for these interests can also be thought of as obligations to oneself.

In order to clarify this point about the possibility of self-obligations, and especially the possibility of self-obligations taking priority over obligations to others, it would be well to sketch two possible moral situations in which self-obligations play important roles. The first sketch is the relatively simple one of three people on a lifeboat, all of whom place value on human life. However, the food situation is such that only one has any likelihood of surviving. Rather than have all starve, some decision has to be made as to which one of the three is to be chosen. Two of the men are older, in their seventies, while the other is in his twenties. Under the circumstances, the younger man argues that on (their and his) moral grounds his survival must be given priority. Very reluctantly, the other two agree.

The point of this sketch is not to develop or advocate a specific moral position. Rather, whether or not one agrees with the humanitarian morality of the three lifeboat occupants, it is to determine if they are handling their problem on moral grounds. Thus, if it were to happen that only the younger man could decide what to do, and if, further, he decided to save himself, was forced to act as the agent as well by literally throwing the others overboard, and do all he could to save his own life, he could, the argument is, still be spoken of as acting on moral grounds. There may, of course, be overriding reasons why the younger man should not choose to save his own life. For one, he may be a captain who has taken an oath to do all he can to help others no matter what their age or condition. Nevertheless, if the conditions are right it would be possible for him to save his own life and to do so as a duty or obligation (i.e., on moral grounds) rather than as an act of self-interest. In this sense he might be spoken of as having a duty to himself.[8]

The second sketch concerning self-obligation is a bit more complicated but shows how one might actually develop a whole moral position around such concepts as self-obligation and self-interest. Imagine the case of Albert (Sketch 10 again) who feels (for our purposes it matters not whether what he feels is correct) that modern society has become too socialistic and people too dependent upon one another. To counteract these "unfortunate tendencies,"

8. By making a distinction between self-regarding duties and duties to oneself, some philosophers (e.g., Singer in his *Generalization in Ethics*, pp. 316–319) have argued that this type of argument merely proves that we can have duties or obligations *regarding* ourselves; but not duties or obligations *to* ourselves. When a person has duties regarding himself, so the argument goes, he is acting on behalf of himself. But to have a duty or obligation to oneself is to *owe* something to oneself in the sense of having contracted with oneself (by way of a promise, etc.). Yet how can one promise himself something if, as both the person who made the alleged promise and the one to whom the promise has been made, he can release himself from the promise? In short, what kind of a promise is a self-promise if a person can get out of it whenever he wishes?

In answering those who have argued along these lines, I would not deny the validity of the distinction between self-regarding duties and obligations, on the one hand, and what I would prefer to call contractual duties or obligations, on the other. I would merely argue that usage dictates that notions of self-obligation and perhaps duties to oneself apply to both of these concepts. Thus in a situation in which a person neglects his own interests for the good of others, it makes perfectly good sense to say to him, "But you have obligations to yourself," quite apart from whether he had ever promised, or could have promised, himself to look after his own interests.

he argues for the principle of self-reliance. Provided each person is given a fair chance, Albert thinks, it is best for the individual and society, in the long run, to look out after his or its *own* interests. He believes this in part as the result of taking competitive sports activities as the model for a person's life pattern. Albert sees how competition strengthens the individual. But his sports model aside, Albert argues that each man's *main* moral responsibility is to himself simply because he, being himself, is in the best position to carry out that responsibility. His moral system, he feels, is simply more efficient than others. He has a fancy theory about the psychological and physical distance between the agent and the patient. The "distance," he says, between the agent and the patient should be kept at a minimum. It stands to reason, his argument continues, that a person (as an agent) is most able to do more for himself (as a patient) than any other person, since he never has to go anyplace to help himself. Obligations to ourselves are not only possible for Albert; because of his Principle of Minimal Distance, such obligations have a priority over obligations to others.

Albert applies his principle of self-obligations not only in the well-ordered society but also to times of chaos. When we say "Every man for himself" as a ship is sinking, this represents not the abandonment of ethical principles but merely a new application of his same principles. It is at this point that Albert differs from his friend Billy who feels that the modern world is in chaos generally and, therefore, that morality is dead. Billy, he says, confuses the loss of the old Turn-the-Other-Cheek morality with the loss of morality. The fact that people may or may not be following certain rules has nothing to do with whether they should be following rules. To Albert's mind, his system of the primacy of self-obligations over obligations to others works better both in and out of the ordered society. In the ordered society it breeds excellence, out of it, it encourages survival.

Again, as with the sketch concerned with the three

men on the lifeboat, the intent in looking at Albert's system of morality is not to encourage approval or disapproval of it. Rather it is to determine whether it is a possible position, for those who would argue against self-obligations would have to argue that it is logically (not necessarily morally) flawed in some respects. But notice how Albert's theory satisfies the principle of generality. Quite in accordance with what Toulmin says, it makes no reference to certain people so as to turn it into theory of privilege rather than ethics. Notice also how it can account for the encompassing feature of ethics (point two above). Although the theory gives priority to self-obligations, it does so only by giving a general reason for this priority; and even then it does not ignore the notion of obligations to others totally. All it does is give priority to self-obligations in a way which permits everyone to receive consideration without necessarily implying that they must be treated equally (point three above). It does then satisfy many of the criteria of a moral theory, enough of them apparently to receive serious consideration as a moral theory rather than one of self-interest or something else.

5. *Political, social, and moral situations*

The intent of this chapter has been to contrast moral with certain non-moral value situations which can easily be confused with the moral, in order to gain insight into moral situations. One of the key points of contrast uncovered has to do with how moral situations exclude and are excluded by the non-moral. In essence, the relationships of exclusion are as follows: Even though a situation involves one's self-interests, if it also involves one morally it is a moral situation; and only if a situation is shown not to be a moral situation can it be either a strictly personal or a self-interest one. In short, one cannot be in both a moral situation, on the one hand, *and* either a strictly personal or a self-interest one, on the other. But even if these relationships hold for all, or a very large number, of moral, self-interest, and strictly personal situations, the question arises whether comparable relationships hold when moral situations are contrasted to still other non-moral value situations. One type which comes obviously to mind, and which will serve to suggest a pattern for other types, is a political (and/or social) situation.

The following might be taken as an example of such a political situation or problem. At its convention The Party is occupied with choosing its candidate for The Presidency. The choice is between Able and Baker. Of the two Able is by far the most qualified for the candidacy, but Baker has the connections and the money. Not surprisingly, Baker gets the nomination, to the dismay of the idealists at the convention. One of these idealists is heard being told by a professional politician, "Look, you're not in Sunday School."

Clearly if what the professional is saying is taken at face value, he is not telling the idealist anything designed to startle him. "Look, you're not in Sunday School" is most likely meant to tell the idealist less about where he is and more about the realities of life. These realities might pertain to the way people behave. If the idealist has lived a sheltered existence, learning about the immorality or un-fairness of others may be startling to him. But if this is the lesson to be learned, our idealist may decide to redouble his efforts to right the (moral) wrongs he has just learned about, and thereby still imply that this political situation is also a moral situation.

However, the politician may not have been concerned just to teach the idealist the political facts of life. In saying "Look, this is not Sunday School," he may not merely mean "This is a rough game we're playing and we often break the rules," but rather "There is no room for (your moral) rules in this game. This is a totally different game." ("Politics is politics," "Business is business," and presumably "Morality is morality").

Whatever the lesson might be, whether it be "Politicians are immoral more often than not" or "Morality has no place in so-called political situations," the idealist's reaction to the politician's comments and the situation in general can be quite revealing. As has already been mentioned, the idealist could respond to the former lesson by redoubling his efforts to reform the party. This sort of response to the situation could be understandable even on the politician's own way of thinking. If the politician's lesson is merely that he and his friends act immorally in making political decisions, then both the politician and the idealist agree about the moral nature of the situation with which they are dealing. Where they disagree is in how to deal with it. The politician, although he vaguely realizes the relevance of moral reasons to the choice of a presidential candidate, prefers to act on the basis of "partisan politics." Thus he supports Baker because Baker will take care of him and his friends after election day. To admit all this is, from the viewpoint of the idealist, to be treating a moral situation as if it were a self-interest one. This then is not only an admission of immorality on Baker's part, but further an argument which begins to destroy the validity of the second interpretation of the lesson being taught by the politician.

In admitting that he and his type voted for Baker in order to line their own pockets, the politician has said nothing to prove his claim that moral rules, appeals, and so forth have no place here in politics. All he has proven is that he and his friends do not in fact appeal to these rules but do instead to one's of self-interest. "Why," the idealist might argue, "should not moral rules and principles be applied to the situation of choosing a candidate?" Why indeed! There are agents (the politicians), actions (choosing the candidate), patients (presumably the people), conditions of value (welfare of the people), and even rules ("We should choose the best man always") present in the situation as there are in the moral situations analyzed already. There is present even the classic conflict of duty and interest; and with respect to this conflict, it at least sounds plausible to say that the former has priority over the latter. Even if the politician refuses outright to grant that the process of selecting a presidential candidate is a moral (as well as a political) matter, we seem to understand and sympathize with the idealist's opposition to this refusal. Once the idealist points out that people will suffer under a bad president, the politician's appeal just to *his* own self-interests sounds inappropriate. In order for the politician to restore the appropriateness of his self-interest argument, it would seem as if he would have to show somehow that people would not suffer under a bad president, their suffering is not a negative value, or something of the kind. And actually he might be able to prove something along this line. But in doing so he would be returning to the moral level. In other words, his claim that morality has no place in political situations, if this is his claim, seems defensible *only if* he can show these situations to be devoid of any moral implications.

Thus it seems that when there are moral implications present in political (and social) situations, they in effect become moral situations. If this is so, one must then reason in these situations as he would in any other moral situation. In one sense, of course, these situations can still be called political (or social) situations as well. Nevertheless, whatever other considerations might be present in these political situations—whether they be political, economic, personal, or what have you—give way to or come to be treated as moral. The moral has priority. Again as with the self-interest situations, this does not mean that these non-moral considerations are excluded; for in the sense explained already, moral situation encompass all these considerations. Thus if the idealist at the Party Convention were to have his way, the politician's interests would not necessarily be ignored. Nor would the interests of the politician's friends. Nor would the Party's political interests. However, although they would not necessarily be ignored, they would be put in a context of some rule or rules so that everyone's interests would be taken into account. The Party then acting (morally) on behalf of the people would, to the extent that the politicians belong to the class of people, be acting on behalf of the politicians. So although a political situation which had moral implications in it might still be called a political situation, it could also, and in a more fundamental sense, be called a moral situation. Moral situations, perhaps not universally but certainly quite generally, seem to possess the characteristic of priority over other situations, and further to have this characteristic, in part at least, because of their encompassing feature.

V.
THE ROLES OF LANGUAGE IN MORAL SITUATIONS

1. Agent-centered uses of language

Until now little mention has been made of the use of language in moral situations. What has been said already pertains mainly to how rules and principles are used in these situations. But as important as these language uses are, there are many others which are equally important and therefore deserve analysis.

The general framework in which it will be useful to look at the many uses of language is that of the agent, patient, and judge of Chapter II. In fact, most of them cannot be understood without reference to these distinctions. One such use is promise making. Promise making is an agent, not a patient- or judge-centered concept. To be sure, one who promises is not an agent to begin with. Yet by making a promise he in effect makes himself an agent; for he commits himself by his verbal performance or act to do or omit from doing something in the future.[1] Prior to saying "I

---

1. "Suppose, for example, that in the course of a marriage ceremony I say, as people will, 'I do'—(sc. take this woman to be my lawful wedded wife). Or again, suppose that I tread on your toe and say 'I apologize'. Or again, suppose that I have the bottle of champagne in my hand and say 'I name this ship the *Queen Elizabeth*'. Or suppose I say 'I bet you sixpence it will rain tomorrow'. In all these cases it would be absurd to regard the thing that I say as a report of the performance of the action which is undoubtedly done—the action of betting, or christening, or apologizing. We should say rather that, in saying what I do, I

promise to . . . " or something of the kind, there may not even have been a moral situation present. The promise making then cannot only literally help create a moral situation, as when someone goes out of his way to meet a friend simply because that friend promised to be there, but at the same time it can create a role for the one who makes the promise as the agent who must *do* what he promised.

At this point the need for distinguishing an action like a promise, which makes an obligation, from an action like carrying out the promise, which satisfies that obligation, becomes evident. Although these two types of action are different in that the former gets us entangled in obligations and duties, while the latter disentangles us, they can both be performed by verbal and non-verbal actions. In addition to verbally promising to do something and thus become entangled, a person can become entangled as an agent, for example, simply by (non-verbally) kicking someone and thereby causing him harm.[2] Similarly, becoming disentangled or uninvolved may be accomplished (non-verbally) by a payment of an amount of money commensurate with the damage done, or (verbally) by an apology.

In addition to promising, a use of language which creates an agent by binding him to do something, and apologizing, a use which unbinds him, there are other uses of language in moral situations which are agent-centered in a different way. A wife (Sketch 11) who is concerned with her own and her children's welfare because of her husband's gambling tendencies and who says to him, "Please honey, you really *must* stop this gambling!" is, as any husband knows, no longer just playing the passive patient's role. Rather she has evaluated the situation and therefore

---

actually perform that action. When I say 'I name this ship the *Queen Elizabeth*' I do not describe the christening ceremony, I actually perform the christening; and when I say 'I do' (sc. take this woman to be my lawful wedded wife), I am not reporting on a marriage, I am indulging in it." J. L. Austin, "Performative Utterances", *Philosophical Papers* (Oxford: Clarendon Press, 1961), p. 222.

2. *Ibid.,* p. 224

is also acting as a judge. In addition, she is using language persuasively, since her words are intended to help move her husband to action. Thus, she is playing the agent's role as well.[3]

Now the differences between the wife's using language persuasively and the husband's using language to make a promise need to be explored in order to avoid confusion about the various roles the agent plays in moral situations. As was just mentioned, the promise makes the husband obligated where he was not obligated before. This is so even though his wife could argue that he had a duty or obligation to stop gambling before he specifically promised to do so. The promise serves, as it were, to bind him further, since his promise is now an additional reason why he should stop his gambling. In contrast, his wife's persuasive words do not bind her to do something in the future. She is not an agent in the sense of placing herself in a situation pertaining to what she ought to do, but rather in the sense of what she is literally doing (i.e., persuading her husband to stop gambling).

There is another way of looking at and thereby appreciating more fully the difference between the wife's and the husband's roles as agents. Although in one sense of the word both are in the same moral situation, since both are dealing with the problem of eliminating her husband's gambling tendencies, strictly speaking there are two moral situations here rather than one. Actually there are three, and it is interesting to note the relationships which hold between them. First, there is the obligation most people would say is present for the husband not to gamble away his family's funds, quite apart from any specific promises he might have made to stop gambling. This obligation, like the promise to stop gambling, may (or may not) have its basis in other promises made (e.g., during the wedding ceremony). Second, there is the promise to stop gambling which creates a further obligation and thereby creates a

3. C. L. Stevenson, *Ethics and Language, op. cit.*, pp. 139–140.

separate moral situation. Finally, there is the wife's decision to use persuasion to get her husband to stop gambling. This now forms a separate and third moral situation.
It is separate from the promise-making, since we can admit
that indeed the husband *ought to* stop gambling because
he promised to do so, but that the wife *ought not* to use
persuasion to bring about this cessation (because she ought
to let him make the decision himself for once). The fact
that the reasons used to justify the two actions, the husband's and the wife's, are different shows that the two
actions, and therefore the two situations, are actually
different. Yet although the reasons are different they are
not totally different, thereby suggesting that the two situations are tied in with one another somehow.

The nature of the tie-in is as follows. One reason the
wife might give to justify her use of persuasion is that
there are good moral reasons for bringing about the end to
her husband's gambling. In her eyes, her use of persuasive
language is a means toward achieving a moral end, since
the morality of her situation (persuasion) is in part at least
dependent upon the (im)morality of her husband's (gambling).

This point can be made clearer by contrasting the above
wife-husband type of problem, in which the wife might be
thought to have solid moral grounds for practicing persuasion, with one in which her grounds might not be quite so
solid. Assume now that the wife has succeeded in getting
her husband to buy her a fur coat which she hardly needs
(as she already has a very nice one) by spicing her arguments with tears and such common moral words as "duty,"
"ought," and "obligation." In this new situation one has a
tendency to think less of the wife than before. But, to repeat an oft-repeated point, the problem here is not to evaluate her morally as such. Rather it is to concentrate upon
identifying the nature of a moral situation—not to judge
it. Part of answering the "What is a moral situation?"
question, however, concerns the various roles agents play
in moral situations and the relationships these roles have

to one another. Thus, quite apart from whether persuasion should morally be practiced in the gambling but not in the fur coat situation, these two examples suggest the following relationships:

1. Other things being equal, if someone is being persuaded to perform a moral act, the persuasive act itself is (becomes) moral.
2. Other things being equal, if someone is being persuaded to perform an immoral act, the persuasive act itself is (becomes) immoral.

These relationships are not moral ones in the sense of being general kinds of moral claims. Rather they are "logical" relationships which show the dependency one type of moral situation has upon another. This dependency is based upon the fact that, although persuading is an act which itself can be morally evaluated, it is also an act which cannot logically be understood without reference to another act—the act one is being persuaded to do. Yet since the two acts, the persuading and persuaded, are different, the moral reasons used to justify each act are different to some extent. As a result, one cannot say that the persuasion is moral simply if the persuaded act is moral. If, for example, the wife succeeds in persuading her husband to stop gambling, her very persuasive actions may undermine what confidence the husband has in himself. This may in turn make him realize how incapable he is of acting on his own and thereby, alas, lead him from gambling to drink. No matter how moral the persuaded action may be, then, whether it concerns basic human rights or not, logically the persuader must still show, before he can practice his persuasion morally, that his persuasion will not bring more harm than good. In other words, it will not be enough for him simply to point to the morality of the persuaded act to justify his persuasion. He will, somehow, *also* have to point to the morality of his own persuasive actions.

Thus far, three different uses of language centered around the agent in a moral situation have been at least partly analyzed. The first, promise making, helps create a moral situation and literally makes a person an agent where he was not one before. The second, apologizing, helps to "break" rather than "make" a moral situation. It is a verbal performance which under the proper circumstances one is obliged to perform. One chooses to make a promise, but he is forced, as it were, to apologize. The third, persuasion, is characterized less for the effect in status it has in the moral situation on the (persuasive) user of language as for the effect it has on others. Further, in contrast both to promise making, a process which creates agents but does not necessarily move them into action, and to apologizing, which retires them, persuading is concerned with getting others (and occasionally ourselves) in motion. It is concerned with either activating agents or making agents out of people in the sense of moving otherwise inactive people to act.

In addition to these three agent-centered uses of language in moral situations, there are other uses which might be thought of as variations on basic themes. Taking an oath, for example, is like promise making, only somewhat more formal. It is also, in some contexts, more binding than a promise. On the other hand, announcing an intention often is less binding than a promise but still, once made, is thought of as having some binding force. Offering condolences and expressing sorrow are also like apologizing except that, as in the case of a death in the family, there is often no suggestion of some previous wrong doing being rectified by the offering or expression. Even persuasion permits of variations. The key to the use of persuasive language is, through its very use, to get someone to do something. However, one can bring this about by using language which is seductive, frightening, sly, misleading, deceptive, or anger-arousing. Further, as any advertiser knows, persuasion can be achieved through repetition and association. But these types are less variations of a basic use of language in moral and other situations than they are various types or forms of persuasion. Still, there are some uses which share with persuasion the characteristic of moving others into actions but are themselves not forms of persuasion. One such is threats. In part, the use of language to threaten someone differs from the use to frighten him in that, with a threat, language is being used as a vehicle to *inform* another what he is threatened with. A threat like "I will shoot you if you don't co-operate" thus, in addition to moving one into action, has an affinity to a promise or an announcement of an intention in being a performative. Until the speaker makes the threat, like making a promise, the listener has not been threatened. The use of language to frighten someone, on the other hand, is a variant persuasive use of language. Here words are used, words which evoke emotion and feeling in the listener so that once he hears them, he is (causally) moved to do what the persuader wants him to do. Whereas a threat, then, is an announcement or pronouncement, a persuasive use like "frightening talk" is a stimulant or a prod.[4]

Another use in the same family as a threat is a command. One who commands must utter (or express somehow) his command as he would a promise. The performance or act is necessary for the command to take hold. But the change of status as the result of issuing the command is not with the speaker (as it is with a promise) but rather with the one commanded. In all these uses—persuasion, threats, commands—it is often an open question as to who the agent is, the speaker or the one spoken to. In some situations when the persuasion is persistent, the threat serious enough, and the command from one in absolute authority, the speaker and not the one spoken to is the agent. The latter person might better be thought of as an instrument of the former under these circumstances. As

---

4. In his *The Revolution in Ethical Theory* (New York: Oxford, 1966), George C. Kerner makes some of these same kinds of distinctions. On the performative side are assertions, commands, etc. while on the "causal" or "prodding" side are uses of language designed to persuade, horrify and do good, among others. See his chapter on Stephen Toulmin, especially pages 116–118.

one might say if he were a private commanded or threatened by a military general to man the trenches, "I had no choice." And where one has no choice, he has no agency. In other situations in which the persuasion, threats, and commands are not quite so dominating, the role of agency would probably have to be shared by the speaker and the one spoken to.

2. Patient-centered uses of language

Just as there are distinctive uses of language for the agent in a moral situation, so it might be thought that there are some for the patient as well. Even if there were—and I will argue that there are not—they would have to be more limited in scope, since the patient, as the recipient of action, plays a more passive role in the moral situation than the agent. If, for example, a patient in a moral situation pleads persuasively to have something done for him, then his pleading turns him into one of the agents or even *the* agent in the moral situation as well. Although, since *as* a patient or recipient of some action the patient cannot plead his case, it might be thought that he can at least make a request. But even in making a request it is not altogether clear whether he is actually playing the patient's role. His request as a verbal performance is intended to get the agent to act. The speaker might be making a request, rather than persuading, because the agent is already disposed to serve the patient. The request, therefore, could serve as a reminder for the agent to get on with the task. Or it could serve as a signal (e.g., "Do it now") informing the agent when to perform the expected action. In part, then, the difference between persuading and requesting is that the former is more concerned with moving someone by changing him, the latter by informing him.[5] In persuading, the greater the change as a result of the persuading, the less inclined we are to call the so-called agent an

5. R. M. Hare, *The Language of Morals* (Oxford: Clarendon Press, 1952), p. 13.

agent, and the more inclined we are to call the persuader the agent instead. However, with requesting, since the change in the agent is minimal at best, it does not seem implausible to still consider the patient (the one making the request) a patient and not an agent.

Unfortunately, there are two considerations which have to be cleared away before requests can be accepted as verbal activity typical of patients. The first is concerned with what precedes the request. Before saying something like "Please help me!" the patient, or someone else, has to make a rational or irrational assessment of the situation. If indeed the patient sees himself as one who should receive some attention from someone, then he again is acting in a non-patient capacity. This is not to say that there is anything morally or methodologically wrong with playing two, three, or more roles in a moral situation. Still, insofar as a person assesses his own or someone else's situation, he is acting as a judge rather than a patient. So now it begins to look as if the use of language to make requests is more akin to the judge's than the patient's function. This too is misleading. As will be seen shortly, the judge's use of language in moral situations results in judgments of the form "You ought to do so and so," "That is the right thing to do," "That was a good move," among others. These judgments may or may not be expressed publicly. Requests, which presuppose such judgments, are public by their very nature. In making a request one must publicly say something like "Please!" "Would you?" or "I wish you would . . . !" A request, then, is not a use of language in a moral situation which expresses the judgment made of that situation as such, but is an additional verbal performance to the judgment. It can, as a result, still be thought of as a possible patient-centered use of language, since it is not reducible to a judge-centered use.

However, the second of the two considerations mentioned above eliminates this possibility. Making a request is not the exclusive preserve of the patient. A patient may be silent with respect to what is his due. He may be unable to talk, as a new born child, or unwilling to do so because of pride or some other such factor. In any case, someone may then act on his behalf and make a request. Such a person would in all likelihood judge the situation but, again, his request on behalf of someone else would be an additional performance which is not really a part of the judgment. So the person making a request is not acting as a judge, nor need he "act" as a patient, and he certainly cannot act as an agent (for he does not make others act or literally move others to action but merely asks them).[6] Since he need not fall under any of these categories, but still since requesting is most closely tied to the patient, his use of language in moral situations can be thought of as a patient-associated use. Thus, to summarize, requesting is better thought of as a *patient-associated* rather than a *patient-centered* use since: 1) others besides patients can make requests; 2) requests are made on behalf of patients; and 3) patients need not make requests to be patients. To make a bad pun, patients can be patient and not say anything.

If this analysis is correct, no distinctively patient-centered use of language has been uncovered as yet. Pleading, although it appeared as if it might be such a use, turned out instead to be more akin to persuading and therefore more in line with the functions of the agent rather than the patient. Requesting also turns out to be neither a necessary nor a sufficient condition for characterizing a patient. However, there is still another possibility in so-called emotive uses of language. When one expresses elation he may not only jump up, raise his hands, and exhibit happy facial features, he may also utter such verbal expressions as "Wonderful!" "Thank goodness!" or "Wow!" Strictly speaking, these "uses" are not uses of language in the

6. In one sense someone making a request in behalf of another may indeed be an agent. Of course he cannot be an agent with respect to the act requested. But making a request is itself an act which one may have promised to perform. I may have promised John to ask George to pay back the money he owes John. George is the agent with respect to moneys owed. But I am the agent with respect to carrying out a promise to ask George about the money.

senses already discussed. In using language persuasively, for example, the agent uses language deliberately to achieve some end. In contrast, emotive "uses" are emitted. Instead of being *released by* the speaker, the words a person utters can more accurately be spoken of as *escaping from* him.

In a way, these emotive "uses" can be thought of as characterizing the patient. As the receiver of some action, good or bad, he is likely to react by expressing some emotion, and as a part of doing so, say something emotively. But, as with requesting, he need not react in this prescribed way. A child may be unaware of what an adult has done for him. Even if he later comes to appreciate what was done, he still may not express any emotions about the matter. Further, those who are not patients in a moral situation, such as bystanders, may find themselves expressing their emotions both in action in general and with words in particular. Even the agent who might be using language persuasively at first may find himself carried away by his own performance and, as a consequence, begin using language emotively. So again no distinctively patient-centered use of language has been found, appearances to the contrary. At best emotive uses might be thought of as another type of patient-associated use.

However, there is yet one final language use which shows promise of fitting the bill as a distinctively patient-centered use. Pleading and requesting are verbal uses *preceding* the action in a moral situation which is evaluated as good or bad. Emotive uses usually, although not always, *accompany* the action. But now *following* the performance of the appropriate action, people occasionally say things like "Thank you!" Rare as it might be, such a use would seem to be patient-associated at the very least. Although, as with requesting uses, saying "Thank you!" is neither necessary nor a sufficient condition for making one a patient, it would seem appropriate for either the patient or someone associated with him (e.g., a parent of the patient) to utter these magic words. Clearly it would not do for the agent to thank himself. Nor is thanking an activity a judge would perform as such. Rather, like requesting, it would seem to be an additional (public) performance to the judgment proper.

If in the sense mentioned above thanking someone is a patient-associated use of language, in another and more basic sense it is also an agent's use. As was just mentioned, the person who has performed as an agent cannot thank himself. Yet once the patient has been acted upon by the agent, a new moral situation can be thought of as having developed so that now the patient has become the agent and the agent the patient. After all, when we fail to thank someone for doing us a good turn, such claims as "Well at least he should have said something" or "What a thoughtless . . . he is" show that thanking someone is an action or performance which can be expected of us as agents (and former patients). So again and finally, distinctively patient-centered uses of language simply do not seem to exist. At best there are only patient-associated uses. This is not surprising in view of the already noted point about the patient's passivity or receptivity in moral situations. The contrast here between the agent and the patient is clear. If a person is not already an agent, the (active) use of persuasive language is sufficient to make him one. For the patient, no such sufficient or even necessary uses exist.

3. Judge-centered uses of language

But what now of the judge? What, if any, uses of language are there which are distinctive with him? In view of some of the distinctions made already, certain uses should be excluded insofar as they reflect functions of the judge in the strictly legal sense of the word but not in the sense being discussed here. In the legal sense, of course, a judge may not even judge a case before him, since he may leave the question of the guilt or innocence of an accused up to the jury. In addition, the court judge has certain functions which might better be characterized as ritualistic or performative rather than judgmental. When he says publicly,

"I commit you . . . ," "I sentence you . . . ," or "I release you . . . ," his actions can be understood better in terms of the agent rather than the judge. Indeed, the court judge's verbal performances or announcements may be *based upon* a judgment made by himself, the jury, or some other authority; but they themselves are not judgments. Rather like commands, promises, or expressions of thanks, these performances are verbal actions which have the effect of literally changing the moral (and legal) situation. Thus, before the judge says "I sentence you to ten years at hard labor," Sticky Fingers is not technically committed to a ten-year stretch. After the judge says "I sentence you . . . ," but not of course just because he says so, Mr. Fingers' life is radically altered from what it would have been had the judge been more lenient and said, "I release you to the custody of your mother."

In this sense of changing the situation, judgmental uses of language do not change the situation. A judge, *not* in the legal sense of the word, need not literally be a participant in the moral situation when he uses language to make a moral judgment. This contrasts with promissory, persuasive, commanding, pleading, and the legal uses mentioned above which unavoidably make one a participant because they affect the moral situation. The point is that although the judge (of a moral situation) may take some verbal action on the basis of his judgment, his judging a moral situation in and of itself is not an action which changes the original or creates a new moral situation. It is not as if judging a moral situation creates a new obligation as the act of promising does.

If distinctively judgmental uses, if there are any, do *not* serve to bind, release, praise, announce, persuade, express thanks, command, advise, and so forth, what then is their function? Clearly it can only be to decide on the rightness or wrongness of a moral situation or moral situations. And although in some general sense this use can be thought of as *one,* several sub-uses or aspects of this overall use can be distinguished. One such sub-use or aspect is for stating

alternative solutions to a moral problem; another is for
stating facts gathered in the process of seeking solutions;
and still another is for classifying these facts. A fourth is
for citing rules and principles, while a fifth is for the formulation of rules and principles. A sixth phase or use of
language within the general category of judgmental uses is
for expressing the final judgment about the moral situation. There may very well be other sub-uses. Nevertheless,
these six, and whatever others may be added to the list,
taken together, have the function or purpose of yielding a
judgment of the moral situation. As such they can be
thought of not only as uses of language within the framework of a moral situation, but also as uses which reflect the
steps one can take to solve his moral problems; that is, the
steps he takes in acting as a (rational) judge.

4. Relations between various uses

Having found certain distinctive uses of language in
moral situations for the judge and for the agent, but not
for the patient, the next problem is to determine whether
these uses have any relationships with one another. That
some relationship(s) exist can be seen from the disturbed
feelings we experience when we hear of someone like Rouser (Sketch 12) employ persuasive and therefore an agent's
use of language (e.g., by using such words as "nigger" and
"tribal invasion") prior to, or in place of, the judge's use of
language. There are several good (logical) reasons for being disturbed with what he does. However, the concept of
a range-rule needs to be introduced prior to presenting an
account of the first of these reasons.

A judge, in the (rational) sense to be discussed shortly,
must be a judge of all aspects of a moral situation. Quite
naturally the aspect which receives the most attention is
the action which is supposed to take or has taken place.
One reason we often focus on the action is simply that in
many moral situations we know who the agent and the
patient are. Under these circumstances, the question is
simply one of deciding what to do, or perhaps whether

what was done to someone by somebody was something good, bad, or indifferent. But in focusing on the action, in judging the situation because we already know who the agents and patients are, we often forget that this knowledge of the agent and patient must have been gained at some other time. Either, when we make a judgment about a moral situation, we must think of it not simply in terms of the action but of the action performed *by* someone *on* someone else; or the action, the choice of an agent (also the judge), and the choice of the patient should be thought of as separate areas about which judgments in the total moral situation can be made.

In favor of this latter interpretation is the following kind of consideration. Quite apart from what is done, we frequently decide separately who is to perform the action and also for whom something must be done. Consider these examples: Quite apart from what a parent does, we feel that the parent, not the neighbor, the teacher, or even the preacher, must act as an agent in handling a child. The father or the mother must do the punishing under certain circumstances, not anyone else. Similarly, officers in the military are agents in the sense of having the responsibility for leading their men in as yet unspecified future battles. In civilian life, citizens are asked to carry out such responsibilities as sitting on juries and voting. But the questions of who are the citizens and/or which ones (whether all or some) should sit on a jury (or vote) can be thought of as separate questions. Thus it seems that there is not just one question to be answered in each moral situation but rather a host of questions, no matter how simple or complex that situation might be. There is, first of all, the question of what should be (or should not be) done. Second, there is often (perhaps always) the question of who should judge a particular situation. This second question can be broken down into two sub-questions: a) whose decision is going to lead the agent into action? and b) who has the right to judge the situation in the abstract or as detached observer?

Third, there is the question of who is the agent; and finally who is the patient?

As is suggested in the above examples of parents, officer, and citizens, often we decide to answer one or more of these questions without deciding how they all should be answered. Thus, if the power of the judge and the agent is given to only certain members of the groups (e.g., those who are over twenty-one years of age and with five years of experience) a kind of moral rule has been established. Since the rule does not tell us directly what action the chosen group will take, but does tell us the *range* or the number of people involved in the moral situation as agents, patients, and judges, these rules can be called range-rules.[7]

Now to return to Rouser and his habit of using persuasion prior to judging the situation through the use of reason. Since dealing with the moral situation is not only a matter of what should be done, but who should judge the situation and act as an agent in it, Rouser's persuasion can now be seen as a kind of action which short-circuits the process of answering these latter two questions. Insofar as he gives some reasons during his persuasive sessions for what he thinks ought to be done, he might be thought of by a stretch of the imagination to be acting reasonably. However, in effect, what Rouser has done as a persuader is to pre-empt, without discussion, other peoples' rights as agents and judges in the moral situation. If, then, each person in the neighborhood group has the right to judge the issue of integration on his own, and as an agent also has the right to take legal action to bring about or delay integration in his neighborhood as he sees fit, Rouser's persuasion can destroy these rights. What it does, if effective, is turn each citizen who is supposed to judge and act on his own into a tool for Rouser, who now alone or mainly is "judging" and acting.

7. N. Fotion, "Range Rules in Moral Contexts," *Mind,* Vol. LXXII. No. 288 (Oct. 1963) pp. 556–561.

Insofar as Rouser is depriving others of their rights, his own persuasive behavior can be judged on moral grounds. However, the main point here is not a moral one but rather one more related to the philosophic question "What is a moral situation?" Part of answering this question has turned on understanding the distinctions between agent, patient, and judge; and part of understanding these distinctions rests on understanding the relationships which hold between them. Since part of the problem in dealing with a moral situation involves a decision as to who are the agent, judge, and patient, (reasonable) decisions about these matters are short-circuited when someone like Rouser becomes persuasive and thereby automatically makes himself the agent as the first step in dealing with the moral situation. Decisions about what ought to be done can also be short-circuited by Rouser's action. In fact, if the persuader is so effective in his persuasion that he persuades even himself, then rational judgments of all aspects of the moral situation become impossible. This means that if both the judge's and the agent's roles need to be exercised in a moral situation, the former must be exercised first. It must be exercised first if for no other reason than that it does not pre-empt or short-circuit the agent's role. After all, in judging a situation, the situation itself is not changed in any way. In contrast, when one persuades, threatens, promises, or employs any of the agent's uses of language discussed earlier in this chapter, he does literally change the situation. In fact, he may change it enough to not only short-circuit the judge's function, but even create a new situation altogether (e.g., as when some naive soul promises to marry the girl someone else has gotten in trouble).

The claim that the judge's role does not pre-empt, but can be pre-empted by, the agent's needs to be qualified. If whoever judges a situation takes an inordinate amount of time to judge the various aspects of that situation, so long in fact that the action cannot be performed at all, then he is affecting the moral situation by apparently pre-empting the agent's role. Actually what he is doing is becoming the agent either intentionally or unintentionally. When a committee chairman prevents the legislature as a whole from considering certain legislation by holding prolonged hearings to judge the merits of a certain program, he is blocking that legislation and *is* acting as an agent. Similarly, if one debates too long whether to save a drowning man, there may not be anyone to save. So there are limits to the point about the judge's role not short-circuiting the agent's. Usually we take these limits into account and in so doing keep the general point about the judge's role not affecting the situation from being invalidated. In emergency situations, when time is short and the situation cannot be judged adequately *after* the emergency develops, we do not abandon the judge's function. Rather, if we are wise, we take steps to judge the situation *in advance,* thereby preparing ourselves for action when the emergency arises.

To prevent any misunderstanding about what has been said concerning the judge's role in the moral situation, it is necessary to make explicit the three-fold ambiguity of "judge." This word was discussed initially in Chapter II in terms of the one whose "judgment" counted in guiding the agent into action. Such a person was spoken of there as the one whose judgment, decision, choice, and so on counted quite apart from whether his "judgment" was rational or not. So long as it was his "judgment" which guided the agent, even if he acted on whim, he was said to be the judge in that particular situation.

Somewhat later in Chapter II this first sense (J1) was contrasted to a second (J2) or bystander sense of judge. Like a J1, a J2 may or may not be rational in making a judgment of a moral situation. However, his judgment, or expression of opinion as it might more accurately be expressed, is not a universal and therefore is not a necessary part of the situation (as J1's sense may be) since presumably a moral situation can develop and be dealt with quite nicely without any bystanders being present.

In this chapter, in contrast, the analysis has revolved around a third (J3), more rational, sense of "judge." To be a judge in this sense one must either be a J1 or a J2; that is, if one is a judge he must be either a judge in the participant sense (J1) or the bystander sense (J2). In addition, he may, in ways which are to be specified in the next chapter, give reasons to back his judgments and, in so doing, qualify as a J3. Clearly this sense of judge is not necessary to a moral situation either, for there are many moral situations (like Rouser's) in which the only judges present are of an irrational J1 type. It is important enough to note the existence of and appreciate the dangers involved in this type of judge. However, the main reason for analyzing cases like Rouser's is neither to note their existence nor appreciate their dangers, but to suggest further that they should be eliminated. In fact, one of the most important reasons for seeking an answer to "What is a moral situation?" is just to show how irrational J1 type judges can be changed into the J3 types.

This conclusion may seem surprising in view of the writer's announced intention to avoid making outright moral commitments in this study. It may be surprising, for now it appears that in answering "What is a moral situation?"— specifically in answering the portion of this question dealing with judges—it is important to say things like "People should deal with problems rationally," "We ought to give reasons to back our moral decisions," and even "We ought not to act on whim in moral situations." All this seems to turn this study from a descriptive account of the nature of moral situations into a prescriptive account of what we ought to do. In other words, instead of just talking about judges and judgments *in* moral situations as he said he would, the author appears to be turning himself into a judge *of* moral situations by actually making moral judgments—his initial denials to the contrary.

However, appearances are sometimes deceptive. The main thrust of this work is and continues to be to answer the question posed originally. A somewhat similar way of asking this same question is "What are the various common or universal *aspects* of a moral situation?" Among

others, those of agent, patient, judge, action, rule, and reason giving have been uncovered and analyzed at least in
part. Yet more than such a reformulation of an original
question is often needed in order to gain a full understanding of its nature. Sometimes it is also instructive to
ask "Of what use is it to answer a particular question?"
The answer to this question is that answering "What is a
moral situation?" is of use to judges (J3) in moral situations. Of course, for some people, notably philosophers, it
may be enough just to answer a question for its own sake
or merely out of philosophic curiosity. But over and above
this, "What is a moral situation?" is a question important
simply because once one answers it through an understanding of the various aspects of a moral situation, and the
relationships they have to one another, he is in a position
of *being a better judge* of what he ought to do. Notice he
is *not* in a position of *knowing* what he ought to do! If he
were, the information he received from answering "What
is a moral situation?" would literally guide his behavior in
a moral situation. This would be tantamount to saying that
in answering this question we should expect to achieve
answers or solutions to the moral situations sketched in
Chapter I. Further, it would be tantamount to saying that
a complete answer to "What is a moral situation?" involves
also a complete answer to any question of the form "What
should I do in such and such a situation?" Actually, far
from achieving a complete answer to this latter question in
successfully achieving a complete answer to the former,
having answers to "What is a moral situation?" in *no* way
gives us an answer to any part of the distinctively moral
question—"What should I do in such and such a (moral)
situation?" What the answer to "What is a moral situation?" gives us is not answers or solutions to problematic
moral situations, but rather an understanding of how to
achieve solutions. Thus a person playing the judge's role is
helped by gaining an understanding of how he moves from
his original role to one of an agent when he shifts gradually from the use of language to help formulate a deci-

sion, to advising uses of language, and finally to persuasive uses. He is also helped when he is made to realize how moral judgments imply general rules and that one would be misled if he thought of moral problems merely in terms "What should I (you, he) do?" rather than also in terms of such range-rule questions as *"Who* should do what should be done?" or even *"Who* should be the judge?" Moral situations are complicated enough so that one interested in the solution to his moral question would do well to look into the question "What is a moral situation?" even though an answer to this question does not literally give us an answer to whatever distinctively moral question we might be facing. Knowing the nature or natures of moral situations at least makes it possible to get the solution to our moral questions by showing us how to get these answers.

It might still be objected that, more than helping judges deal with moral problems, it was claimed earlier that the philosopher of ethics (concerned as he is with such philosophic questions as "What is a moral situation?") might be tempted as a philosopher to say things like "You ought to use reason." To say this, however, seems to turn the philosopher into a moralist once again. "Ought," after all, is a typical moral word, and its use in "You ought to use reason" clearly guides behavior just as any moral rule has been said to do.

In replying to this objection, the distinction mentioned above between guiding someone as to *how he can find a solution* and guiding him by *giving him a solution* should be kept in mind. "You ought to use reason" and like utterances would seem to fall more in the former, the philosophic, rather than the latter, the more moral, category. "You ought to use reason," "You ought to try to formulate some rules here," "You ought to look at all sides of a question," and the like need not then, just because they look grammatically like moral claims, be taken to be such claims. Although the word "ought" ("should," "good," "right") is used in moral situations, this does not mean that it can have no other uses. Indeed it can, and in these cases it is being used to do other than moral duty.

So the philosopher *as* a philosopher can make recommendations, but make them on the level of guiding the judge in his search for solutions to moral questions. Yet this conception of the philosopher as one who gives aid and comfort only to the judge might be thought to be too narrow. Might not the agent and patient also be the recipient of the philosopher's wondrous benefits? Should not, all of us, as it were, benefit? But why not? The conception of the judge as the sole or primary beneficiary is not as narrow as it seems. The judge in a moral situation, especially in the J2 or detached-observer sense of this word, might very well include everyone or almost everyone. For it must be remembered that the concepts of judge, agent, and patient can all be applied to one person at the same time. It is the one who plays the judge's role, however, whose task is really the most complicated, and he is therefore in the best position to profit from philosophical analysis.

VI.
MAKING JUDGMENTS IN
MORAL SITUATIONS

1. Justifying moral judgments

Of all the uses of language mentioned and discussed in the previous chapter, those related in some way or other to the judge seem most complex and difficult to understand. To be sure, an agent (or potential agent) in a moral situation has several uses of language, including persuasion and promise-making, available to him. Yet, however many agent uses of language there are, they seem to be distinct from and unrelated to one another. It is not as if in playing the agent's role one must first make a promise and then follow it up with such an agent-centered use of language as persuasion. In contrast, the uses of language for purposes of judging (J3) must be related to one another. So closely are they tied to one another that it is an open question whether it is best to talk of one general use (much as one would speak of one team playing together) or of several different uses. Further, so closely are they tied to one another that serious misunderstanding of the judge's role is likely to develop if one is not clear as to what the various "steps" in the judging process are, and how these steps are related to one another.

In Chapter III, three levels concerned with the process of reason giving were distinguished. One level or step was factual reason giving. A second was reason giving as it pertained to citing and "making" rules, while the third was reason giving as it pertained to citing or making value judgments. Although in Chapter III these reason giving steps were not explicitly shown to be related to the judge or the judge's role in a moral situation, it should be clear now that they are so related. Starting then with these three steps, the question which naturally comes to mind is: Which of the three is the first, the second, and the third step in the process of acting as a judge (J3) in a moral situation?

In Chapter III certain relationships between these three steps in the process of judging were discussed without being stated in one-two-three form. One such relationship was between factual reasons and moral rules—more specifically, a relationship which shows how the latter help make the former relevant to a moral situation. A fact can be shown to be relevant in a discussion about a moral situation, it was suggested in Chapter III, when it can be shown to fall under some rule. Thus statements of fact concerned with a shooting, beating, carrying away another's property, lying, or thoughtlessness are generally relevant in a moral discussion, because most of us try to live under rules which prohibit these activities. Indeed, without some rule to which to appeal, it is difficult to imagine just where one would start in describing a moral situation or how he would identify it as a moral situation in the first place. One knows he is in a moral situation, at least in part, because he observes some behavior which he thinks is right or wrong—or expects someone to perform some right or wrong act at a certain moment in time. But an act is right or wrong because of some feature it possesses or some connection it has to some other fact or consequence. Therefore, if it is right or wrong for these reasons, similar acts will be right or wrong for the same reasons. In making judgments about right and wrong, in other words, one is appealing to rules, one purpose of which is to filter out a small amount of data as "relevant" from the vast amount which comes our way. Without these rules, any and all data would be as relevant or irrelevant as any other, and it would therefore be difficult to know where to start. So at least on one level of reasoning about moral problems, factual reasons are relevant in moral situations because rules make them relevant. Presumably, one could cite factual reasons to justify some action only *after* he had appealed to or cited certain moral rules.

More will be said about the relationship to facts to rules later. Analysis of certain contexts or levels of moral problem solving will suggest an actual reversal of the order of appeal, since the facts will be cited *before* the rules are even formulated. For now, in order to prepare the way for understanding this reversal of order, it is necessary to discuss at length what relationships exist between moral rules and value judgments made in moral situations. One way of raising the question of these relationships is to ask again, only in a somewhat different way, what moral rules and value judgments are. When these questions were asked in Chapter III, moral rules and value judgments were contrasted in terms of the former's "guiding" and the latter's "goal-stating" functions. Rules literally guide behavior by telling us what to do (e.g., not to steal, kill, slap, or hit; and to help or be considerate of others) while value judgments direct us in the sense of giving direction to behavior (e.g., seek happiness, maximize pleasure). Whereas, in some contexts at least, rules are helpful in showing us how to reach a goal, value judgments have the function of setting the goals for us in the first place. This manner of stating the relationship between the rules and the judgments already suggests that the latter must be decided upon before the former.

Raising the questions again about the nature of moral rules and value judgments confirms this suggestion. If one were asked to give examples of moral rules, he could respond with "Don't kill" or perhaps even "Be kind." If he did so, his response would highlight the guiding function of such rules, since, in the form stated, these rules simply tell us either what behavior to refrain from or what behavior to exhibit.

In this form, however, these rules can mislead us, since in highlighting what is or is not to be done they omit mention of what must be implied in a full understanding of these rules about agents and patients. The rule is never, when fully stated, simply "Don't kill" but rather "You (we, they) should not kill him (them)." Reference to the agent and the patient, in other words, is implied in the shorthand statement of the rule. If this is so, the application of the rule or the rule itself must imply further that decisions (range-rules) have been made as to who are the agents and the patients. But to say this, especially with respect to the patient, is at least indirectly to say what is valued. One is a patient not merely because a promise has been made in "his" direction. The recipient of a promise is someone or something of value. Part of what makes a promise for (or to) a child binding, for example, even if the child does not understand language, is that the one who makes the promise (or someone else) places value on the child itself, its experiences, or some other aspect of the child. Similarly, in following rules such as "Don't steal" and "Don't kill" it is difficult to understand what force these rules would have if the patients to which they applied were not property owners, alive, and so forth, but also were not valued in and of themselves (or for some of the characteristics which they possess in and of themselves). It is difficult to imagine, in other words, how one could talk about using a rule to justify an action without, in the end, justifying the rule in terms of some value judgment. Moral rules are not just guidelines for any action; presumably they guide the action of an agent on behalf of creatures which we value.

So there is a sense in which there is a one-two-three order in the sequence of appeals in justifying an action or proposed action. The first step which is necessary or presupposed before either one of the other two appeals can be made is the appeal to a value judgment. Having made this appeal, it is logically possible to appeal to rules and, in turn, to facts. Actually, although this is the *logical* order of appeal, the order is often reversed in practical justification.

Logically the argument is that when we attempt to justify an action or proposed action, the facts we cite must in principle be relevant *to* some value judgment. In practice, however, since we often share moral convictions (i.e., rules, principles, and value judgments) with those with whom we have moral discussions, we frequently start these discussions on the factual level. Since a husband and a wife share, hopefully, many views about life, it is quite natural to suppose that if they disagree about what to do in a certain situation the disagreement will rest on a factual basis. Such would be the case if a husband were to come home and reprimand his wife for not doing her duty in cleaning and ordering the house, when she and one of the children have been sick all day. The problem of assessing the reprimand in this situation is resolved quite simply by informing the husband about the situation. Although this minor problem is resolved first and last by means of an appeal to facts, one should not be misled into thinking that this is all there is to the situation. Hidden in the background, presupposed in the sense of having been decided upon at some other time, are the rules about a wife's duties and of the value a person places on his spouse and other human beings in general.

These presuppositions can and do at times come out into the open. When they do, this usually is a sign of a crisis situation. The need to start a discussion arises when there is a question of what one should do when a discussion on the factual level fails. If a husband agrees with the wife that it is a strain on her to do all the housework even though she has a job out of the home as well (Sketch 8), and if at the same time he coldly says "So what?" they are in for trouble. When she cites the strain she is operating under, she is presupposing a rule which might be expressed, "Share and share alike." If he, on the other hand, agrees with the fact that she is operating under a strain but, let us suppose, feels it is a dangerous precedent to have the male indulge in housework, her facts are irrelevant to him, since his rule concerned with the role of the husband in the home is different from hers. What they might do to settle their problems is find some other rule or value judgment upon which they agree, which in turn may be cited to get one or the other party to change his mind on the original rule. Whether this or some other procedure is used, the argument is clearly now on the rule and perhaps value judgment level; and it got there *after* the discussion had started and became stalemated on the factual level. Still and all, to repeat, in justifying what one does or does not do, it remains true that logically the rules and value judgments must precede, in the sense of presuppose, the factual appeal no matter on what level the justification may have begun in actual practice.

2. Formulating moral judgments

In contrast to *justification,* there is a different level of moral reasoning which may be called *formulation.* As it has been described here, justification is actually a process on the second-order level, one dependent upon the formulative process. In spite of this fact, it is probably a process used more frequently than the formulative. The case of the husband who refuses to do housework shows why (Sketch 8 again). He, keep in mind, gets along quite well with his wife except on the sticky matter of housework. This getting along is quite understandable, since both were raised in the same socio-economic milieu—raising which presumably breeds similar opinions, attitudes, prejudices, and behavioral patterns. Given this similar background, it is not likely that they will have to spend an inordinate amount of time with one another formulating rules. They are more likely to be justifying their actions by appealing to already formulated rules. To be sure, their rules need not have been formulated in any conscious sense in their minds. In all likelihood, instead, they would have been handed down to them by their society through the process of conditioning, and are expressed now by them in the form of habits of behavior and almost unconscious attitudes and opinions. This situation of sharing a common background is hardly unique. Most people, no doubt, are raised in and live out their lives within one culture. This being so, two people raised in a common culture (or a group raised in one culture) might very well achieve a crisis-free existence through the expedient of not challenging any of the basic precepts of their common heritage. Problems for them would be mainly ones of justification, since they would appeal to already formulated and ordered rules in order to "justify" whatever stand they may have taken with respect to a question. One could, in fact, imagine a fairly static society in which the members of the group, for generations at a time, would rely almost completely upon justification rather than formulation to deal with their daily moral problems.

As opposed to this, if one were living in a rapidly changing society or, more radically, if he were to pull up roots and settle *outside* his own society altogether, he might find the process of justification inadequate for dealing with his problems. It might no longer be adequate to cite certain rules, since these rules might not be honored by The Outsider's adopted group. This does not necessarily mean that the rules he cites, if he does so, are inappropriate, wrong, or anything of the kind. But it does mean that he will be forced to defend his rules. In defending these rules he might cite other rules or value judgments to see if he has some point of contact with his new society. This would be to make a move akin to what the unhappy couple made when they could not solve their housekeeping problems. But such a move presupposes much common ground in moral thinking, and such common ground may not be present. Let us suppose, for example, that The Outsider finds himself among people who have sexual practices quite different from his, make promises but do not keep them often, have many more exceptions to the prohibition of killing than merely self-defense, and value far more than he does the physical pleasures of life. Surely the temptation (understatement) would be for him to rethink his whole conception of life and to appeal not merely to principles and rules accepted in the past, but to think of why these principles and rules were formulated in the first place. At this point it would do no good to say that his reformulation is merely a more persistent form of justification as this word has been used (somewhat technically) here. Indeed, The Outsider can carry out a more or a less complete analysis of his moral rules, principles, value judgments, and so forth and, in this sense, justify some proposed or past actions. Further, he would undoubtedly carry out such a process as a preliminary step to engaging in the formulative process of moralizing. Yet sooner or later, either gradually or suddenly, he would probably find himself not defending or justifying what he already holds in terms of an appeal to something else he already holds, but wondering seriously if he had better not rethink his whole conception of what things are right and wrong, good or bad.

This sort of basic rethinking could happen as the result of a radical culture change (as with The Outsider), a war, or a personal catastrophe. It could also happen just because someone, anyone, wants to rethink his moral stand on life as a sort of theoretical exercise. Nevertheless, the fact that it is more likely to happen in a crisis situation suggests something different about the process of (re)formulation in contrast to justification. Whereas the latter presupposes rules before facts can be cited for justification, the former presupposes facts before rules can be formulated. Presumably what one must do when he is in moral shock, since (many, most, or all of) his rules, principles, and value judgments are in question, is work with all that remains—facts.[1] This is perhaps another way of saying that in order to formulate moral rules, and from these go on to formulate some moral system, he must live a little.

In this connection, it is often said in books on ethics that a certain amount of experience is needed before it is advisable to engage in the study of ethics. Although he was not

---

1. Used in the broad sense so as to include scientific laws, theories, etc.

so much concerned with the study of ethics as such as he was with making sound judgments in ethics and political science, Aristotle put it as follows:

> Now each man judges well the things he knows, and of these he is a good judge. And so the man who has been educated in a subject is a good judge of that subject, and the man who has received an allround education is a good judge in general. Hence a young man is not a proper hearer of lectures on political science; for he is inexperienced in the actions that occur in life, but its discussion starts from these and are about these; and, further, since he tends to follow his passions, his study will be vain and unprofitable, because the end aimed at is not knowledge but action. And it makes no difference whether he is young in years or youthful in character; the defect does not depend on time, but on his living, and pursuing each successive object, as passion directs. For to such persons, as to the incontinent, knowledge brings no profit; but to those who desire and act in accordance with a rational principle knowledge about such matters will be of great benefit.[2]

Aristotle would have us experienced not only in knowing about the world (its facts) but also presumably in judging it (by uncovering its moral rules and values). Indeed, this condition is similar to that of The Outsider just before he left his old group. First, he had available to him a vast fund of data about the world—including all of its creatures; and, second, he had past experience in judging right and wrong, good and bad. His problem, however, was in having had experiences which made him wonder about the correctness of his past judgments. In such a condition he had to face the problem of formulating rules, principles, and of making value judgments without presumably appealing to rules, principles, and value judgments in the first place. Prior to his departure he was in the following state:

2. Aristotle, *Nicomachean Ethics,* 1094 b-29 to 1095 a-12. (McKeon translation). Random House, N.Y. (1941).

1. He had read some Freud and was suddenly surprised to discover how little effect The Rational Principle plays in man's (his own included) life and how large The Irrational Principle does;

2. He had recently been sent to the hospital as the result of being beaten up by some Strong Arm Storm Troopers;

3. He had also just heard of the death of his best friend in the Ten-Or-More Years War;

4. Finally, he had heard of such news as the marriage of his friend's sister, the return of his lost billfold (with the money in it), the politeness of a stranger who said "Thank you" when someone helped her lift a heavy suitcase.

But how, the question arises, could The Outsider have made any moral decisions and rise out of his moral skepticism if he could not justify his decisions by an appeal to some rule or value judgment? In the special sense of "justify" being used here, he could not, for "justify" means literally appealing to some rule, principle, or value judgment. What he would have had to do is formulate some rules or make value judgments.

One traditional answer as to how he could have done this is the theory of intuitionism. Often this theory is presented as a way of dealing with all or most moral decisions; or at least it is not made clear at just what point or how often in the process of deciding what to do one is supposed to appeal to an intuition. If the distinction between justification and formulation is a valid one, it would *not* be necessary to appeal to an intuition in all problematic moral situations. The reason for this is that once formulated (intuited) the rule could be appealed to as a way of justifying a decision without necessarily calling up the intuition each and every time.

However frequently or infrequently one is supposed to appeal to an intuition, the role of the intuition in the problem-solving situation is a decisive one. On this theory, the intuition permits us to be immediately aware of the rightness (or wrongness) of some action, value, or rule and thereby to formulate or generate other value judgments, rules, or even a moral system. As it is usually conceived, both the intuitive powers which man is supposed to possess and the objects intuited are thought of as unique in the sense of not being reducible to or analyzable into sense intuitions or objects of sense (such as qualities of green, having pleasure, or empirical facts). What the intuitionist wants to argue for is that at the crucial formulative or generative level such sentences as "That is good" or "That is right" cannot mean anything descriptive such as "That is pleasant" or "That is desired." At this generative level, to say "X is good" (or "X is right") is, over and above discovering it to be pleasant, for example, *also* to discover it to possess certain moral qualities,[3] relations, or "facts".[4] Thus, for the intuitionist there may come a time in a moral situation when a *judge* cannot merely describe that situation, nor can he merely justify his or someone else's actions in that situation, by appealing to already accepted rules and value judgments. What he must do in addition is intuit—discover or uncover—an objective moral truth which will either be a rule or value judgment itself, or will lead to the formulation of a rule or the making of a general value judgment based upon the discovered moral truth.

Such intuitionists (objectivists, non-naturalists, or non-reductionists) are opposed by others traditionally called naturalists.[5] Again the level upon which these differences in ethical theory lie should be clear. The dispute, to put it linguistically, is not on the level of the patient's or the agent's uses of language. As the patient was found to have no distinctive uses of language within moral situations, there is no real problem here. But with the agent, the

3. G. E. Moore, *Principia Ethica.* See Chapter I.
4. E. W. Hall, *What Is Value?* (New York: The Humanities Press, 1952), pp. 247–249, 225–226.
5. See, for example, R. B. Perry's *General Theory of Value* (New York: Longmans, Green and Co., 1926, or the Harvard University Press, 1950), Chapter V.

dispute between the objectivist and the naturalist has nothing to do with the persuasive use of language in moral situations. Neither side need deny that "That is good," "That is the right thing to do," and so forth might be used persuasively or in any of the other agent's ways of using language discussed in Chapter V. Nor even on the judge's level need they dispute about how a decision is to be justified. What they are disputing about does indeed have to do with the judge. Specifically it has to do with how the judge formulates or generates rules and/or value judgments; and what the naturalist says is that in formulating rules or value judgments no special intuition or objects of intuition are needed. All we need appeal to, according to the naturalist, is our natural feelings, desires, inclinations, attitudes, or pleasures.

Thus, depending upon the specific form the naturalistic theory takes, moral language is used either to refer to natural qualities or relations, or to assert natural facts about ourselves or some aspect(s) of the situation. According to the naturalist, when one approaches the generative or formulative stage of dealing with moral problems (i.e., when he can no longer appeal to what he has held onto in the past as right or good), the only appeal he has left to help develop his position is to such natural experiences as pleasure and desire. At this generative level, to say "X is good" (or "I ought to do X," etc.) means literally "I like X" (or some such natural equivalent as "We have a positive attitude toward X"). In presenting such a definition and thereby reducing moral to so-called natural terms, the naturalist need not commit himself to saying that the definition he is presenting applies to other non-moral contexts or to other aspects of the overall moral situation. When someone says "X is good" and, in so doing, gets someone else to do something, the "meaning" or "use" is persuasive and may have nothing to do with the generative meaning or use of the same utterance. Even the judge's use of "X is good" at the justifying level of moral reasoning may not mean what the naturalist says it means on the generative level. At the latter level, "X is good" could mean "I like X"; while at the justificatory level it could mean "We have accepted X as something we should strive for."

Although the naturalist is not committed to applying his definition to other than the generative level of problem solving, neither is he committed to denying that his definition may apply to other levels of problem solving or non-judgmental uses of language. Quite apart from whether a person is using moral language at the generative level, he might say "X is good" (or make some other moral claim) and mean "I like it" (i.e., mean what the naturalist means by "X is good" on the generative level). All the naturalist *is* committed to is a proposed definition for the generative level of problem solving, quite apart from what "X is good" and the like might mean in any other context.

There is another traditional position which claims to characterize the generative level of dealing with moral problems. If instead of saying that expressions like "X is good" refer to unique moral qualities, relations, or assert unique moral facts, or refer to natural qualities or relations or assert natural facts, one says that there is no referring or asserting here at all, he is close to adhering to the emotive theory. All he needs to add to hold onto this theory is to say that expressions like "good" and "X is good" are merely emotive emissions.[6] Instead of describing anything (natural or non-natural) when uttered on the generative level, an expression like "X is good" is taken by the emotivist to be a piece of behavior which is (emotively) emitted along with such other pieces of behavior as raising one's arms, jumping up and down, increasing the heart beat, and the like.

Concerning these three theories—of intuitionism, naturalism, and emotivism—the following three comments are appropriate. First, since the issues surrounding the matter of deciding between them are extremely complex, there is

6. A. J. Ayer, *Language, Truth and Logic* (New York: Dover, 1952). See Chapter III.

time to show only the level upon which the issue must be settled. To repeat, it does no good at all in attempting to refute the intuitionist to point to any aspect of the moral situation other than the judge's use of language at the generative level. At any other level or in any other context such expressions as "X is good" may not refer to or assert anything uniquely moral, since at these other levels and contexts "X is good" can be used to persuade, describe something other than something uniquely moral, and so forth. Similarly, if one is concerned with refuting or supporting the naturalist or emotivist, he must express his concern on the same generative level. Second, if the intuitionist is right, there is no arguing for or against the position. Presumably once all the irrelevant issues (e.g., agent's uses of language) surrounding the question of the intuitionist's theory are cleared away, one either (directly) intuits these qualities, relations, or moral facts, or he does not.[7] It is not a limitation of the theory that one cannot argue for it. It is hardly fitting, therefore, to say that the theory is bankrupt since it cannot be rationally defended.[8] Rather it is the nature of the theory that whatever it is which is uniquely moral is directly intuited. One similarly does not argue for the other positions. If there is nothing uniquely moral to intuit, then one immediately sees either that moral words refer to or moral sentences assert something natural, or the words refer to and the sentences assert nothing at all. Where the arguing takes place is in the preliminary clearing away of the debris surrounding the issue (e.g., confusing commending, commanding, promising, and advising uses of language with what I have been calling the formulative or generative ones). Third, if the intuitionist is right, what was said in Chapter III about the possibility of moral situations not having a unique moral element would turn out to be wrong after all.

7. H. A. Prichard, "Does Moral Philosophy Rest on a Mistake?" *Readings in Ethical Theory*, edited by Sellars and Hospers (New York: Appleton–Century–Crofts, Inc.), pp. 149–162.

8. G. Warnock in *Contemporary Moral Philosophy* (New York: St. Martin's Press, 1967) hits the intuitionists on this point. See pages 12–17.

VII.
SUMMARY AND CONCLUSIONS

While summarizing certain key points discussed in the previous chapters, certain other points will be made in this chapter concerning the role of the philosopher of ethics in (and/or out of) moral situations. In Chapter II, after discussing the roles of agents, patients, and judges, all of whom were said to be a part of the moral situation in one way or another, the moral philosopher was said to be apart from it. However, the exact sense in which he could be said to be apart from moral situations was not specified in that chapter. Nor was it specified completely in Chapter V how the philosopher of ethics (or moral philosopher) was said to be of service mainly to the judge in the moral situation. In that chapter he was said to be of service to the judge not by giving him solutions to moral problems, but by giving directions as to how he might achieve solutions. Even having said this much, it is still not clear whether this is all the philosopher of ethics can do. Can he, in spite of what has been said, become somehow a part of the moral situation as well?

Notice, first of all, the sense in which the patient has been said to be a part of the moral situation. He is the recipient of the agent's act. More than that, the agent's act affects him in some morally significant way (e.g., by giving him pleasure, causing him pain). The patient is a part of the moral situation in the sense then that he is the one on behalf of whom the agent is acting, when the agent is acting as he should; or he is the one the agent is doing something *to,* when the agent is acting as he should not. There are also people in moral situations who can be called patients because they should be receiving attention (but are not) from agents who are "sleeping on the job." In any case, the patient is literally a part of the moral situation in so far as without him it would be difficult to say what a moral situation is all about. Without the patient there would be no moral point to the agent's act.

Similarly, without the agent, the one who "operates" on the patient, it again would seem difficult to imagine what a moral situation is all about. Without him there could still be conditions or things of value. Even though no one could do anything about an earthquake, for example, the conditions of suffering which such an event can bring about might very well be considered terrible. But still, so long as no one can do anything about the earthquake—that is, so long as there is no agent present—there can be no (moral) patient (although there would be sufferers) and no moral situation. The agent is a part of the situation, then, since his actions or capabilities for action help turn a situation which may be merely one of value into one of moral value.

The role(s) of the judge in the moral situation is complicated by the three senses of "judge" distinguished in Chapter V. J1-type judges are literally a part of the moral situation, since by definition their decisions are the ones which count in directing the agent's actions. However, since the agent can often act on habit (i.e., non-thinkingly), it may be misleading to say that a judge even in the J1 sense is necessary for every moral situation. One would think that if he were acting on habit now, he would at least have had to make judgments in the past in similar situations. However, this seems doubtful. Many actions done on habit now (e.g., always being polite, keeping promises, and never telling lies) are consciously judged or decided upon at some previous time. Yet with many others we act on habit in a way which makes it difficult to trace the habit back to some decision. The child, the parent says, has always been honest. The parent himself is like the child. And so on. So, although when one judges a moral situation as a J1 he is a part of the situation, as much so as the agent and patient, it still seems by no means obvious that a judge must be a part of every moral situation.

There should be no misunderstanding here. What I am arguing is that it may be misleading to think of every moral situation as containing at least one judge. However, this does not change the "fact" that in other moral situations judges (J1) are present and are a part of the situation. In this same sense a J2, an "observer," "detached," or "sidelines" judge, obviously is not a part of the moral situation. Nevertheless his judgments are still those (in either the rational or irrational sense) *of* the situation. The same applies to a J3-type judge who is also either a J1 (involved) or a J2 (uninvolved) but who is rational about his decision making. Even judges whom I have called moral thinkers are judges of moral situations and in this sense a part of them. To be sure, moral thinkers look at the general rather than the specific situation. Yet a good part of what they are saying about the general will apply to the specific situation. If a moral thinker comments about the society's sex standards in general terms, complaining that they are too rigid or too loose, his comments can easily have application to the sex standards of an individual in society. So he too, the moral thinker, is a part of the moral situation in the minimal sense that he is a judge of it, at least in the "bystander" sense of the term.

In contrast, the moral philosopher, *as* a moral philosopher, is not even a part of the moral situation in this minimal sense. Since he is not, he seems to be so remote from the moral situation as to raise a real question as to his usefulness to those who are a part of it. The answer already given to this question is that as a moral philosopher, the philosopher can be thought of as of use to no one; or he can be thought of as of use to those who are judges in moral situations insofar as he analyzes such concepts as judge, patient, agent, reason-giving, persuasion, and performative uses of language (e.g., promise-making).

Such help, it was said, would enable the judge to deal with his problems more rationally, since it would help to show him how to find solutions, even though it would not find the actual solutions themselves.

Granting all this help he can give others, the philosopher of ethics must *still* be spoken of as being apart from rather than a part of the moral situation. To see this in the clearest light, it is useful to contrast again the moral philosopher with the judge, since the judge's function as a part of the moral situation most closely approximate the philosopher's. One of the reasons which has not been mentioned until now for confusing their respective functions is that both of them can be spoken of as "engaged in an analysis of the moral situation." The judge, whether he is a J1, J2, J3, a judge of a particular situation, or even a moral thinker, analyzes the situation in order to make a judgment about its goodness, badness, rightness, or wrongness. In order to do this analysis correctly, the judge must assess the relevant facts, moral rules, and values of the situation. He must, that is, determine if the situation is one in which someone has been hurt, and whether in fact this person was hurt by an agent (or whether it was an accident). He must further adopt or maintain some rule about one human hurting another and must judge whether humans and their conditions of life have value. The judge, in other words, is an analyst of the situation by way of *evaluating* it. His final judgment is aimed at such things as guiding the agent's behavior and informing the patient as to what he (morally) ought to expect from the agent.

As an analyst of moral situations, the moral philosopher would seem to be almost on a par with the judge. In fact, the model used in this study is one of first looking at a variety of moral situations and, as a result of this looking, making such distinctions as that of the agent and patient. Thus, insofar as the moral philosopher literally analyzes moral situations also, he too would seem to be involved in them or be a part of them rather than apart from them.

Still, notice what it is the moral philosopher analyzes. Unlike the judge, he is not concerned with assessing the truth or falsity of the relevant factual claims as such (by gathering data). Nor is he directly concerned, as is the judge, with the adoption or maintenance of moral rules; nor even is he directly concerned with making value judgments. Finally, he is not concerned with guiding agents, informing patients of what is to be expected from agents, or anything of the kind. Instead, he can be variously spoken of as analyzing the structure, "logic," the preconditions, or even the "basis" of the moral situation. But all of these expressions are metaphorical, ambiguous, or just downright misleading. It is better to say that instead of analyzing the situation as the judge does, by *assessing* its truth, falsity, rightness, or wrongness as a whole or in part, the moral philosopher analyzes the conditions under which such assessments are or should be made. Whereas the moral philosopher identifies the judge and characterizes his various roles, it is the judge who actually plays one of these roles. Similarly, whereas the moral philosopher characterizes the other participants (the patient, agent, propagandist, adviser, and the like) it is they who are the participants, not the philosopher. So in spite of the fact that he, like the judge, can be spoken of as "an analyst of the moral situation" and is of help to the judge, unlike the judge he is still apart from rather than a part of the situation. His analysis of the situation is of the conditions which make it a moral situation. The judge's analysis is of the actual rightness and wrongness of it.

There are many reasons why people are not prone to accept these conclusions about the moral philosopher. Two of the most important are as follows. First, they forget the distinction between a philosopher acting as a philosopher, and as a parent, citizen, owner or, for that matter, a human being. To say that a philosopher as a philosopher is apart from moral situations is not to say that he cannot be a part of them in any one of the many other roles which he undoubtedly plays in society. As a philosopher, however, he has certain functions to perform which should not be confused with whatever other functions he must perform in carrying out his non-philosophical roles. Again, all these roles may very well be legitimate in one sense or another, but they are different. So, although the philosopher of ethics as a (total) person is not apart from moral situations, he is apart from them when he is on the job.

Second, those who would have the moral philosopher in his capacity as a moral philosopher be a part of moral situations fail often to be aware of a second and lesser known distinction. They confuse being a part of a moral situation *as* (or in the capacity of) a moral philosopher with being a part of a moral situation *because* one is a philosopher. Being a part of a moral situation as a philosopher, I have been arguing, makes no sense finally. The very process of making (and exploring) such concepts as agent, patient, (relevant) reasons, rules, emotive uses, range-rules, and value judgments which characterize the moral philosopher separates him from those who are a part of the moral situation. However, because he is a moral philosopher he *may*, when he does become involved in moral situations, play his role as an agent and judge more effectively than he might otherwise. It is important to stress that he *may* play these roles more effectively, because, although he may be practiced and competent at making certain distinctions as a philosopher, he may not be practiced or competent at applying them in the actual moral situation.

Still, it could be argued that even supposing that moral philosophers *may* be unpracticed and incompetent in applying the concepts they analyze, surely their chances of being better judges are improved because they are moral philosophers. Their familiarity with the agent and judge distinction alone would tend to keep them from making certain mistakes which others might make.

By and large, this argument is a good one. Because moral philosophers engage in moral philosophy they probably are better judges of moral situations—other things being equal. To clinch the conclusion of the argument one would, of course, have to prove it to be true by observation. But there is no reason to suppose it could not be so proved. Yet what if it were? What would it show? That moral philosophers *can* be said to be a part of the moral situation rather than apart from it? Hardly! What it would show is that the things one learns from the moral philosopher when he operates as a moral philosopher have practical application to moral situations. Indeed one would hope they would, otherwise why bother with them? One way in which moral philosophy was said to have practical application is that it helps the judge not in giving him solutions to whatever moral problems he might be facing, but in showing him how to go about finding them. Thus a person who professionally operates as a moral philosopher might very well be a better judge of a moral situation, just because he is a moral philosopher. However, this is not to say that as a moral philosopher he is a judge and therefore a part of the moral situation. Rather it is to say that his operations as a moral philosopher can be used in the separate and independent operation of judging when he is in the position to play that role (instead of the moral philosopher's).

Quite compatible then with the position that a moral philosopher *as a moral philosopher* operates apart from moral situations is the claim that *because* he is a moral philosopher he can be of special use *as a judge* in a moral situation. Yet too much should not be made of this point. *As* a moral philosopher a person is in position to be aware not only of the strengths, but also of the limitations of his discipline. Bringing with him the tools he has developed as a philosopher, he should realize that these "logical" tools alone are not enough to enable him to make rational judgments of a moral situation. He should realize that what is missing is the material upon which the tools can operate—value judgments, moral rules and principles and, finally, general empirical knowledge. The philosopher may, for example, be able to build and use his own logical tools, but he may not be experienced, trained, or have at his command any one of the following items which would keep him from being an effective judge of a moral situation:

1. The knowledge to assess the reliability of a witness' report relevant to determining guilt or innocence (as a lawyer might be better able to);
2. Information as to how a war started and what similarities one war might have with another (as a historian might have);
3. Knowledge of the laws, rules, etc. of a society (as a legal judge, lawyer, or sociologist might have);
4. Practice at appealing to moral rules and principles in a variety of situations (as a minister, psychiatrist, social worker, and legal judge might have);
5. Perspective as to how a criminal (delinquent child, emotionally disturbed person, etc.) will behave when he is given the responsibility of going on his own (as a sociologist, social worker, psychologist might have).

In other words, with respect to these areas of knowledge and others besides, any one of which might be relevant to judging any particular moral situation, the philosopher of ethics would be an amateur. Being an amateur, of course, is not a bad thing; yet being an amateur is not being a professional either.

Most philosophers seem to be aware of their amateur status with respect to data gathering. In fact, they seem to have a real preference for letting others do this sort of work for them, thereby releasing themselves to do the more esoteric theoretical work for which they are noted. But even here, does the moral philosopher's work or training place him in a privileged position to theorize about value judgments, for example? Traditionally, from the times before Socrates and Plato, the philosopher was supposed to be the wise man. This wisdom was not usually expressed in terms of everyday living, but rather in those of the goals or purposes of life (value judgments) and even in terms of what is sometimes called a "philosophy of life."

If the basic argument of this chapter is correct, the philosopher simply is not in a privileged position of making value judgments (or affirming moral rules and principles, for that matter). To put it somewhat paradoxically, the philosopher of ethics is not necessarily, nor even especially, qualified to be a philosopher of life. To be a judge of values, philosopher of life, or however one wishes to put it, involves more than merely being an expert in the analysis of "agent," "patient," and the rest. Nor is it enough to be learned also about a range of such other concepts as life, death, happiness, pleasure, the good life, contentment, or even wisdom. This is not to say, again and finally, that the philosopher cannot be of any help. If the role of the philosopher makes him expert at the business of analyzing concepts, then surely such important concepts as happiness and wisdom could use his careful analysis. But having uttered such useful insights as "Wisdom is something more than knowledge" and "Happiness is a dispositional concept," the philosopher has not as yet told us what it is to be wise or happy. As a conceptual analyst (philosopher of ethics) he simply cannot, for *as* an analyst he does not know what it is to be wise or happy. No more so can he tell us about these things than can the philosopher of science tell us what are the facts of the world because he has explained to us what a fact is (i.e., explained the concept of fact). Similarly, just because it is important for the philosopher of history to be learned about such concepts as time, event, revolution, and evolution does not make him learned about when certain events happened and which revolutions or evolutions were successful, or even which ones took place. And so it goes. If one wishes to place himself in a privileged position of making value judgments, he must be more than an analyst of concepts. In addition he would have to have experienced a wide variety of situations and have judged a wide variety of problems (e.g., how to deal with change, conflict, and women) from a wide variety of points of view. There is little evidence to suppose that the philosopher is any more experienced in these regards than many non-philosophers. In short, some knowledge has been gained here both about the worth *and* the limitations of the philosopher. These may not be unimportant things to know.

ANNOTATED BIBLIOGRAPHY

Ayer, A. J., *Language, Truth and Logic*. Dover Publications, Inc., New York (1952), (Oxford University Press, 1936; 2nd Edition, Victor Gollancz, Ltd., London, 1946), pp. 160.

This famous little book is hardly a treatise on ethics. Nevertheless it deserves to be in a list of ethics books because it contains a forceful defense (in Chapter 6) of the emotive theory of ethics (which treats "moral judgments" more as emotive emissions rather than truths either about the world at large or about the individual). This book is also worth reading since it shows how an ethical (really a meta-ethical or a moral philosopher's) position can develop out of a more general philosophic one.

Baier, Kurt, *The Moral Point of View*. Cornell University Press, Ithaca, New York (1958), pp. 326.

Professor Baier offers his reader a vigorous presentation of the moral point of view within the traditions of linguistic analysis and naturalism. Baier argues that ". . . morality arises out of the relations between people. . . ." As a result of this view and other considerations, he takes an opposite stand on the question of self-obligations (duties) than I do. He argues, for instance, that duties have to do with the "station" one holds within a society. On this basis, it makes little sense to talk about duties to oneself. Even obligations (in contrast to duties) demand a partner. The obligation, therefore, is to the partner, not to oneself.

Binkley, Luther J., *Contemporary Ethics Theories*. Philosophical Library, Inc., New York (1961), pp. 203.

Professor Binkley gives a fair and clear presentation of the last sixty years of the history of ethics. His study is wide in scope in that, in contrast to Kerner and Warnock cited below, he describes and analyzes the writings of a variety of moral philosophers.

Davis, Philip E., *Moral Duty and Legal Responsibility*. Appleton–Century–Crofts, New York (1966), pp. 288.

This is an interesting book especially in relation to Chapter I
of the present work. Although it contains some commentary by
Davis, primarily it presents a series of case studies of a wide
variety of legal problems. In several of the cases, for example,
the question of the relation of law to morality is raised. The case
studies also are of interest in relation to the present work since
they exhibit the methods and procedures of the law.

Ewing, A. C., *Ethics*. English Universities Press, Ltd., London
(1953), pp. 183.

In the process of presenting a fairly up-to-date introduction of
the more "classic" or "traditional" way of doing ethics, Professor
Ewing has written a highly readable little book. Included in this
book is a defense of intuitionism and an attack on utilitarian
(consequential) theories.

Fletcher, Joseph, *Situation Ethics: The New Morality*. The West-
minster Press, Philadelphia (1966), pp. 176.

This is a missionary job and in one sense may not belong in
this list of books on the philosophy of ethics. Dr. Fletcher writes
from a religious rather than a philosophic tradition. His mission
is not to transform non-believers into believers, but believers
who have been shackled by the "terrible literalism and legalism"
of Church ethics into believers who can practice Christian ethics
reasonably. Thus, what most philosophers take for granted, that
rules are guidelines for action and not rigid tracks, Dr. Fletcher
thinks of as revolutionary. In spite of the stress Dr. Fletcher
places on "methodology" which gives this book some philosophic
import, it is still mainly a work which is moralistic in tone. The
tone itself is that of a Christian "love" ethic. The examples of
moral situations he gives along the way are excellent.

Frankena, William K., *Ethics*. Prentice-Hall, Inc., Englewood
Cliffs, New Jersey (1963), pp. 109.

Professor Frankena discusses a wide variety of problem areas
in a short amount of space, including those of the nature of the
distinction between ethics and meta-ethics, the contrast of moral
judgments and value judgments, the number and types of
values there are, the importance of consequences in determining

what is right and wrong, the status of the intuitionist position, and how to justify moral judgments. In the process, Professor Frankena shows himself willing to draw moral conclusions from what look like meta-moral principles which he accepts. In any case, although the book is not as readable as one might suppose it to be for a "beginning" volume, it is rich in pointing to and illuminating many important distinctions.

Hall, Everett W., *What is Value?* The Humanities Press, Inc., New York (1952), pp. 255.

Professor Hall presents *the* most sophisticated version of the objectivist position, a version developed just before this position went out of style. Hall argues that Moore was wrong in thinking of value (e.g., goodness) as a quality. Nor is it a relation. Rather, it seems to be more akin to a (value) fact, and thus is represented linguistically not by words (which typically point to things) or even to phrases but by whole sentences. Like Moore, Hall believes that these value sentences or judgments are irreducible to descriptive sentences or truths. Hall writes within the tradition of the linguistic school of philosophy and maintains, as I do, a sharp distinction between ethics and meta-ethics. *What is Value?* is not an easy book to read but it is rewarding.

Hare, R. M., *The Language of Morals.* Oxford at the Clarendon Press (1952), pp. 202.

This book is already a classic. Hare's concern is to make such important distinctions as those between imperatives (used to *get* people to do something) and moral judgments (used to *tell* people something); commands (addressed to individuals or sets of individuals) and moral judgments (which are generalizable); and descriptive meaning of "good" (which varies from case to case) and the evaluative meaning of "good" (which is constant and has the function of commending). As the title suggests, it is written in the linguistic-analytic tradition.

Hare, R. M., *Freedom and Reason.* Oxford University Press, New York (1965), pp. 228.

Freedom and Reason represents Hare's later thoughts on some of the questions which he discussed in *The Language of Morals.* In particular he is concerned with the question of the extent to which an individual chooses his moral position. Is a person free to choose his basic moral principles or is he subject to reason in a way which restricts his choice? In the end, Hare says that although reason imposes restrictions (e.g., we must be willing to imagine that we are the victims and the victims are the "persecutors" before we act in some situations, in that in ethical matters we do not reason in terms of "for me"), man is still free. All this is not necessarily a happy state of affairs, for this means that the "fanatic" who has ideals diffcrent from the majority cannot be refuted. The fanatic can, in short, hold his position consistently, even if it means death and destruction.

Kerner, George C., *The Revolution in Ethical Theory*. Oxford University Press, New York and Oxford (1966), pp. 254.

Professor Kerner's book is an "analytical" history of twentieth-century moral philosophy with emphasis on the contributions of Moore, Stevenson, Toulmin, and Hare. Kerner argues that each of these writers made a contribution which led to the present level of understanding of ethics; but each was either unclear, or pointed only to a portion of the "truth" as we understand it today. Toulmin, for example, overemphasized the descriptive element in moral judgments and in the process confused (fused) the ethics and meta-ethics distinction. Hare, on the other hand, directed more attention to the evaluative element in moral judgments but gave an oversimple analysis of this element. According to Kerner, moral judgments such as "X is good" are not used merely or mainly for approving (Stevenson) and commending (Hare). Rather they are used to perform a variety of tasks (e.g., grading, ascribing, applauding, congratulating). Although the material in this book is somewhat difficult, it is both rewarding and up-to-date.

MacIntyre, Alasdair, *A Short History of Ethics*. The MacMillan Company, New York (1966), pp. 280.

As the author states, this book is more than a history of ethics. Actually it is an analysis of moral concepts in a historical framework. MacIntyre argues that not only do moral views change in time but also that moral concepts change as well. Differing views of life as expressed in history evidently need differing concepts in order to be expressed. For MacIntyre, even today when there is moral conflict, this conflict expresses itself not only in the different moral rules and values which people hold but also in the concepts which they use to express their views. A consequence of his position is that he would disagree with the conclusions of Chapter VII of the present work. Since for him the concepts one uses are not separable from the moral position one holds, no sharp distinction exists between doing conceptual analysis (meta-ethics) and judging moral situations. His work differs in still another respect from my own. He emphasizes the role of the society in the formation of moral concepts. In this respect, although in my opinion he may be overemphasizing this role, he supplements (rather than disagrees) with some of the things I have been saying about moral situations.

Meldon, A. I., *Ethical Theories: A Book of Readings.* Second Edition, Prentice Hall, Inc., Englewood Cliffs, New Jersey (1955), pp. 496.

This is an excellent book of readings, presenting substantial excerpts from the works of classical writers (Plato, Aristotle, Epicuras, Epictetus, Saint Augustine, Thomas Hobbes, Joseph Butler, David Hume, Immanuel Kant, Jeramy Bentham, John Stuart Mill, Francis Bradley, Henry Sidgwick, G. E. Moore, and H. A. Prichard).

Moore, George Edward, *Principia Ethica.* Cambridge University Press (1903, first edition; reprinted in 1948), pp. 232.

Principia Ethica may be *the* classic of twentieth-century moral philosophy. Although of late it has received much abuse, it is still recognized almost universally as the starting point for twentieth-century moral philosophy. In part the abuse it receives has to do with the particular form of the objectivist (or intuitionist) position for which Moore argues. However, not only do modern writers tend not to think of "good" as referring to a unique, unanalyzable quality which somehow attaches itself to other more natural qualities, they also tend to be unsympathetic with the whole enterprise of objectivism. Quite apart from the abuse, Moore's book is extremely rewarding reading. It includes, for example, a clear discussion of the ethics and meta-ethics distinction and a clear-cut effort to apply the distinction (i.e., to engage in meta-ethics and ethics as separate enterprises).

Nowell-Smith, P. H., *Ethics.* Penguin Books Inc., Baltimore, Maryland (1954), pp. 324.

This is an excellent source book for many issues in ethics;

including some not discussed in the present work (e.g., freedom, responsibility, conscience). It is also an excellent book with respect to the many uses to which moral language can be put (although it was published somewhat too early to incorporate the concept of performatory uses).

Prior, Arthur N., *Logic and the Basis of Ethics*. Oxford University Press (1949), pp. 111.
   This is a useful little book in giving the reader perspective into the history of the naturalist and non-naturalist issue. Professor Prior views Moore's contributions to this issue not as revolutionary but rather as carrying on a tradition which goes back at least to the seventeenth and eighteenth centuries, and to such writers as Cudworth, Hutcheson, Hume, Reid, and Sidgwick. Prior says not only is Moore's claim that naturalists commit the "naturalistic fallacy" (of trying to define ethical words in terms of descriptive ones) not original; but, he adds, this claim or argument belongs in the larger context of the alleged fallacy of trying to prove ethical conclusions from non-ethical premises. Since this larger question is still discussed by philosophers (see MacIntyre's book cited previously) Prior's book is still worth reading even if one is not interested in the history of the philosophy of ethics as such.

Sellars, Wilfrid and Hospers, John, *Readings in Ethical Theory*. Appleton–Century–Crofts, Inc., New York (1952), pp. 707.
   Although somewhat dated, this volume still contains the best sampling of articles and excerpts on recent developments in ethics found between two covers. It includes writings in defense of the intuitionist (Sidgwick, Moore, Prichard, Ross, and Ewing), naturalist (Dewey, Perry) and emotivist (Ayer, Stevenson) positions. Further, it contains articles on such questions as the relation of duty to interest, the nature of free will, and the problem of justification. Since the last twenty years has seen progress made especially in the latter area, it is here that the Hospers-Sellars volume shows itself to be most dated.

Singer, Marcus George, *Generalization in Ethics*. Alfred A. Knopf, New York (1961), pp. 351.
   Professor Singer gives a detailed analysis of the nature of the process of generalizing in ethics and the conditions under which

it is applied. Singer considers what he calls the Generization Principle (". . . what is right . . . for one person must be right . . . for any similar person in similar circumstances." p. 5) and other principles, rules and arguments derivable from it to be moral (rather than meta-moral) in nature. I would, of course, disagree with this classification. He also differs with the stand taken in the present volume on self-obligations. Singer asks, how can anyone be expected to be obligated to himself by way of a promise when, as the one to whom the promise has been made, this person can (if he so desires) release himself from the obligation? These differences aside, Professor Singer has good discussions as to why such reasons as "You are an American" or "I like it" fail to satisfy one or the other of his generalization principles, and thus fail to be proper backings for moral judgments. He also has good discussions of the conditions under which the Generalization Principle should not be applied.

Stevenson, Charles L., *Ethics and Language*. Yale University Press (1944), pp. 338.

In attempting to show the practical import of ethics, Professor Stevenson makes a distinction between the descriptive and emotive meanings, both of which moral terms and judgments possess. It is emotive meaning, not descriptive meaning (the language of science) which has the primary task for Stevenson of making morality practical. Words and other expressions have an emotive impact upon people, moving them to do things which they otherwise would not be inclined to do. The fact that expressions with emotive meaning can move people to action leads Stevenson to stress the persuasive and propagandistic uses to which moral language can be put. With respect to moral disagreements, Stevenson argues that only those based on fact have a rational basis for resolution. Disagreements of (basic) attitude are not in principle resolvable by rational means. Thus persuasion (verbal and otherwise) is the only solution here. For Stevenson, therefore, in contrast to the objectivists (Moore, etc.), morality is subjective at its roots.

Taylor, Paul W., *Problems of Moral Philosophy*. Dickenson Publishing Company Inc., Belmont, California (1967), pp. 517.

The readings (articles and excerpts from larger works) contained in this volume are primarily by twentieth-century writers, although there are selections also from such earlier writers as Hobbes, Butler, Hume, Kant, and Mill. The chapter headings, under each of which three to five selections are clustered, are varied. Paul Taylor's comments preceding each chapter heading are long enough to be informative and yet short enough not to tempt anyone not to read the articles themselves. In addition to discretion, Professor Taylor also has the virtue of being a clear writer.

Toulmin, Stephen E., *An Examination of the Place of Reason in Ethics*. Cambridge, at the University Press (1953), pp. 228.

As the title indicates, Professor Toulmin is anxious to point to the role of reasoning in ethics (after the likes of Stevenson, Ayer, and even Moore made it seem as if reasoning has only a minimal role to play in ethics). For Toulmin, moral discourse has the function of harmonizing the aims of society. Given this function, we can present facts as reasons which support moral conclusions. Toulmin has been criticized, rightly I think, for supposing this harmonizing function to be literally a part of the "logic" of moral discourse. This function is instead probably an expression of Toulmin's own moral position (i.e., a moral, not a meta-moral insight). Nevertheless, Toulmin's book (along with Moore's, Stevenson's, and Hare's) is one of the twentieth-century classics in ethics in that it signals a shift in thinking from one direction to another.

Warnock, G. J., *Contemporary Moral Philosophy*. St. Martin's Press, New York (1967), pp. 81.

In this well written little volume Professor Warnock reviews the recent scene in ethics (starting with Moore) and then goes on to present his own view on the status of ethics—which is a variant of the naturalistic position. In developing his position, he criticizes Hare (much as Kerner does) for giving an overly simplistic view of ethical language. Speech acts used in moral contexts, Warnock says, have such other functions besides pre-scribing, as advising, exhorting, imploring, commanding, and confessing. More to the point of his own naturalistic-like posi-tion, Warnock hits at Hare for putting too much emphasis on the universalizability feature of ethical language. To characterize ethics uniquely, Warnock feels, one must not only talk about universalizability but of some sort of content as well. The relevant content, he thinks, has to do with our desires, wants, and the like; or, to put it differently, with human welfare. As against Hare then, Warnock says that evaluation does not finally rest on choice, for we do not choose what to want or prefer.

Weldon, T. D., *The Vocabulary of Politics.* Penguin Books Inc., Baltimore, Maryland (1953), pp. 199.

Weldon applies the techniques of linguistic analysis to a field related to ethics. Similar to the distinction between ethics and meta-ethics, Weldon marks the distinction between politics and meta-politics. He uses this distinction, along with others, to show how philosophers of politics have made serious mistakes (e.g., into thinking that from an analysis on the meta-political level, political conclusions could be forthcoming). Among other concepts, Weldon analyzes "justice," "the state," "freedom," and "rights." In addition, he has a final chapter on the relation between politics and morals.

INDEX

action(s), 27, 30, 48, 67, 83, 84, 89, 102
advising, 90, 105, 123
advisor, 21, 110
agent(s), 17, 18, 20, 21, 23–27, 29, 30, 38, 48, 50, 53, 64, 67, 70–73, 75–79, 81–87, 89–92, 95, 106–111, 114
agent-centered uses of language, 70–77, 81, 86, 102
apologizing, 71, 75. *See also* performative uses of language
Aristotle, 100, 120
Augustine, Saint, 120
Austin, J. L., 70–71
Ayer, A. J. 104, 116, 121, 123

Baier, Kurt, 2, 51, 54, 56, 116
Bentham, Jeramy, 120
Binkley, Luther J., 116
Bradley, Francis, 120
Butler, Joseph, 120, 123

command, use of language to, 76
commands, 82, 118
commanding, 82, 105, 123. *See also* performative uses of language
commending, 105. *See also* performative uses of language
condition(s), 27, 28, 30, 48, 67, 107
condolences, offering, 75. *See also* performative uses of language
confessing, 123. *See also* performative uses of language

conscience, 121
contentment, 114
creature(s), 26, 28
critic, 19–21, 23, 24. *See also* judge
critic, bystander, 22. *See also* J2-type judge
critic, involved, 22
Cudworth, Ralph, 121

Davis, Philip E., 117
death, 114
Descartes, Rene, 25
Dewey, John, 121
duties, 116
duties to oneself, 56–65. *See also* self-obligations

emotive uses of language, 79, 80, 111
emotivism (emotive theory), 104, 105, 116, 121, 122
encompassing, 54, 59–62, 65, 68
Epictetus, 120
Epicuras, 120
Ewing, A. C., 43, 117, 121
exclusion feature of moral situations, 51, 54–56, 65
exhorting, 123. *See also* performative uses of language

fact(s), 99, 100, 112, 122
facts, relevance to moral situations, 37, 109

factual reason giving, 43
factual reasons, 44, 46
fanaticism, 119
Fletcher, Joseph, 117
formulation, 97–105. *See also* generating rules
Fotion, N., 85
Frankena, William, 17, 44, 117
freedom, 121
frighten, use of language to, 75–76

generalizability, 40. *See also* universalizability
generalization, 33
generating rules, 97–105. *See also* formulation
Generization Principle, 122
God, 25, 26
good life, the, 114

habit, 20
Hall, E. W., 102, 118
happiness, 114
Hare, R. M., 35, 77, 118, 119, 124
Hobbes, Thomas, 120, 123
Hospers, John, 121
human(s), 7, 25, 26, 28, 29
Hume, David, 120, 121, 123
Hutcheson, Francis, 121

imperatives, 118
imploring, 123. *See also* performative uses of language
intention, announcing an, 75
interests, 59
intuitionism (objectivism), 101–105, 117, 118, 120

judge(s), 19–26, 29, 30, 38, 50, 53, 78, 82–84, 86, 87, 89–92, 102, 103, 105, 106, 108, 112. *See also* critic
judge, J1-type, 87–88, 107–109. *See also* pp. 19–26
judge, J2-type, 87–88, 91, 108–109. *See also* critic, bystander
judge, J3-type, 87–89, 92–93, 108–109

judge centered uses of language, 70, 78, 81–83
judge, legal sense of, 81–82
justification, 92–97, 98–99, 101

Kant, Immanuel, 120, 123
Kerner, George C., 76, 116, 119

language in moral situations, Chap. V

MacIntyre, Alasdair, 119, 121
Mayo, Bernard, 23, 25
Meldon, A. I., 120
meta-ethics, 117–120, 124. *See also* meta-moral, moral philosopher, and philosopher of ethics
meta-moral, 122, 123. *See also* meta-ethics, moral philosopher, and philosopher of ethics
meta-politics, 124
Mill, John Stuart, 120, 123
Moore, G. E., 2, 102, 119, 120, 121, 123
moral judgments, 117, 118
moral philosopher, 25, 106, 108, 110, 112, 115, 116. *See also* meta-ethics, meta-moral, and philosopher of ethics
moral reasons, 74
moral rules, 46, 109, 110, 112
moral rules, following, 45
moral situation(s), 1–2, 24, 25, 27, 28–32, 44, 47, 48, 58, 60–61, 72–73, 83–86, 88, 89, 106, 107
moral situation, unproblematic ones, 33
moral situations, general, 33–36
moral situations, particular, 33–36
moral situations, standard ones, 37–38, 41
moral thinker(s), 22, 108, 109. *See also* social thinker

naturalism, 102–104, 105, 121, 123

naturalistic fallacy, 121
non-moral situations, 28
Nowell-Smith, P. H., 120

oath-taking, 75. *See also* performative uses of language

patient(s), 17, 19–21, 23, 24, 26, 27, 29, 30, 38, 48, 50, 51, 53, 64, 67, 77–81, 83–86, 89, 91, 95, 106, 107, 108, 110, 111, 114
patient-associated use of language, 79–81
patient-centered uses of language, 70, 77–81
patient, open-ended feature of, 28
patient's use of language, 102
people, 7, 17
performative uses of language, 70, 71, 108, 121. *See also* apologizing, commanding, commending, confessing, condolences (offering), exhorting, imploring, oath-taking, pleading, prescribing, promising, requesting, sorrow (expressing), thanking, threatening.
Perry, R. B., 102, 121
personal situation(s), 44, 55–56
personal situations (strictly), Chap. IV, 49–54
persons, 26
persuading, 77–78, 80, 82, 83, 85, 90, 92, 105
persuading (persuasive use of language), 71–77
persuaded act, 74
persuasion, 86, 103, 108, 122
persuasion, forms of, 75
philosopher of ethics, 21–25, 28, 88–91, 106, 111, 113, 114. *See also* meta-ethics, meta-moral, moral philosopher
philosopher of science, 29, 114
philosophy of life, 112, 113
picking, 20

Plato, 113, 120
pleading, 77, 79, 80, 82. *See also* performative uses of language
pleasure, 114
political situations, 65–69
prescribing, 123. *See also* performative uses of language
Prichard, H. A., 105, 120, 121
principle(s), 45, 46, 70, 112
principles, moral, 42
principles (moral), holding on to them, 45
Prior, Arthur N., 121
priority feature of moral situations, 50–52, 55–56, 68–69
promise, carrying it out, 71
promises, 82
promising, 70–72, 75, 82, 86, 92, 95, 105. *See also* performative uses of language
propagandist, 110
prudential situation(s), 44, 46, 52–69

range-rule(s), 83–88, 90, 95, 111
reasons, 39, 40
reasons, important ones, 40
reasons, relevant, 35, 40, 111
reasonable, 40
reason-giving, 40, 43, 89, 108
reason-giving, factual, 41, 92–94
reason-giving, moral rule citing, 92–94
reason-giving, value citing, 92–93
recipient, 27
Reid, Thomas, 121
requesting, 77–80. *See also* performative uses of language
responsibility, 121
Ross, David, 121
rule(s), 33, 34, 41, 42, 48, 67, 70, 89, 90, 93, 96–105, 111, 117
rule, acting in accordance with, 36–37, 46
rules, dangers of, 38–40

rule, following a, 36–37, 57
rules, functions of, 36–38
rule-making, 33
rules, moral, 94–97, 100
rule, reason-giving, 43
rules, relevant ones, 93

scientific situation(s), 28–32, 46
self-interest, 52–69
self-interest, appeals to, 55
self-interest situation(s), 57, 58, 60–61
self-obligations, 56–65, 116, 122. *See also* duties to oneself
self-regarding duties, 63. *See also* duties to oneself
Sellars, Wilfrid, 121
Sidgwick, Henry, 120, 121
Singer, George Marcus, 26, 51, 54, 56, 63, 121
social thinker, 22, 25. *See also* moral thinker
Socrates, 113
sorrow, expressing, 75. *See also* performative uses of language
Stevenson, Charles L., 42, 72, 119, 121–123

Taylor, Paul W., 122
thanking, as a use of language, 80, 82. *See also* performative uses of language
thoughtlessness, 18, 27, 93
threatening, 76, 86. *See also* performative uses of language
Toulmin, Stephen E., 2, 58, 119, 123

universalizability, 35–36, 40, 58, 65. *See also* generalizability
utilitarian (consequential) theories, 117

value judgment(s), 40–49, 67, 94–97, 100, 102, 107, 109–114, 117

Warnock, G., 105, 116, 123
Weldon, T. D., 124